YA

KIM
KARDASHIAN

TV PERSONALITY AND BUSINESS MOGUL

KIM KARDASHIAN

TV PERSONALITY AND BUSINESS MOGUL

Dennis Abrams

Enslow Publishing
101 W. 23rd Street
Suite 240
New York, NY 10011
USA
enslow.com

Published in 2019 by Enslow Publishing, LLC.
101 W. 23rd Street, Suite 240, New York, NY 10011

Copyright © 2019 by Enslow Publishing, LLC.

Library of Congress Cataloging-in-Publication Data

Names: Abrams, Dennis, 1960- author.
Title: Kim Kardashian / Dennis Abrams.
Description: New York : Enslow Publishing, 2019. | Series: Influential lives
| Includes bibliographical references and index. | Audience: Grades 7-12.
Identifiers: LCCN 2017016833 | ISBN 9780766092075 (library bound) | ISBN 9781978501751
(paperback)
Subjects: LCSH: Kardashian, Kim, 1980–Juvenile literature. | Television
personalities–United States–Biography–Juvenile literature. |
Celebrities–United States–Biography–Juvenile literature.
Classification: LCC PN1992.4.K345 A38 2017 | DDC 791.4502/8092 [B] –dc23
LC record available at https://lccn.loc.gov/2017016833

Printed in the United States of America

To Our Readers: We have done our best to make sure all websites in this book were active and appropriate when we went to press. However, the author and the publisher have no control over and assume no liability for the material available on those websites or on any websites they may link to. Any comments or suggestions can be sent by e-mail to customerservice@enslow.com.

Photo credits: Cover, p. 3 Vanessa Carvalho/Brazil Photo Press/LatinContent/Getty Images; p. 6 Valerie Macon/Getty Images; p. 11 Manny Carabel/WireImage/Getty Images; pp. 15, 19, 40 Ron Galella/WireImage/Ron Galella Collection/Getty Images; p. 25 Tony Duffy/Allsport/Getty Images; p. 30 Vince Bucci/AFP/Getty Images; p. 36 Alexandra Wyman/WireImage/Getty Images; p. 42 Gregg DeGuire/WireImage/Getty Images; p. 47 John Shearer/WireImage/Getty Images; p. 54 Jeff Vespa/WireImage/Getty Images; p. 58 Michael Bezjian/WireImage/Getty Images; p. 61 Philip Ramey/Corbis Entertainment/Getty Images; p. 66 Jeff Kravitz/FilmMagic/Getty Images; p. 70 Gary Gershoff/WireImage/Getty Images; pp. 75, 101 Kevin Mazur/WireImage/Getty Images; p. 80 Ray Tamarra/Getty Images; p. 84 Christopher Peterson/BuzzFoto/FilmMagic/Getty Images; p. 90 Pascal Le Segretain/Getty Images; p. 93 KCS Presse/Splash News/Newscom; p. 97 Splash News/Glu Mobile/ Newscom; p. 99 Amanda Edwards/WireImage/Getty Images; p. 106 © AP Images; p. 108 Bertrand Rindoff Petroff/French Select/Getty Images; back cover and interior pages background graphic zf-foto/Shutterstock.com.

Contents

Introduction

· · · · · · · · · · · · · · · · ·

S he is one of the most famous women in the world—famous, as they say, for being famous.

She is famous for her beauty, for her body, and, perhaps most notably, for her bountiful rear end.

She is famous for being the star of a hit reality show, which showcases her, her mother, her sisters and brother, and her equally famous stepfather.

She is famous for her boyfriends and her husbands.

She is famous for being the queen of the selfie and has published a 448-page book, *Selfish*, which is a collection of many of her best photos.

She is famous, or infamous, for a private tape she made with an ex-boyfriend, which went very public.

But is that all she is?

· ·

As a successful entrepreneur, Kim Kardashian has risen above claims that she is simply famous for being famous.

Kim Kardashian is also famous for being a master of social media, with 105 million followers on Instagram and more than 50 million on twitter.

She is a hugely successful entrepreneur whose business acumen has given her a net worth estimated at between $50 and 150 million.

She has been named one of the most influential women in the world—one whose Instagram posts and tweets earn her between $25,000 and $350,000 each.

She is married to one of the most famous and influential rappers in the world.

She is a loving mother, devoted to her family.

Born Kimberly Noel Kardashian and now legally Kimberly Kardashian West, she is much more than many give her credit for.

This is her story.

Family History

· ·

Kim Kardashian is the great granddaughter of immigrants who came to America in search of a better life. Her great grandfather Tatos was the child of Protestant Armenians who fled to Russia to escape religious persecution. But Russia did not remain a safe haven for the family. An elder in their village of Karakale warned them that the time had come for all Armenians to leave Russia and settle on the West Coast of the United States. Over a ten-year period, more than two thousand ethnic Armenians made this journey. The Kardashians took his advice and moved to California.

Opportunities in America

Tatos met his soon-to-be bride, Hamas Shakarian, onboard the ship that brought his family to America. They settled in California in 1913. Once there, he opened a garbage collection business that quickly grew into a

On Being Armenian

Kim's Armenian heritage is important to her and to her sisters and brother, in part because it was so important to their father. Every year on her dad's birthday and now on the anniversary of his death, the whole family has dinner at his favorite Armenian restaurant, the Carousel. She's even found a way to use Armenian symbols in some of the jewelry she has designed.

large-scale operation. This business made him and his family a small fortune.

In 1917, his son Arthur was born. In 1938, Arthur married another émigré from Armenia, Helen Arkenian. The Kardashian family business had now expanded to meatpacking. When the United States entered World War II in 1941, the military contracts they earned made the Kardashians' company a great deal of money.

Business was so good, in fact, that the family members were multimillionaires when Kim Kardashian's father, Robert, was born to Arthur and Helen in February 1944. Robert and his brother Tommy grew up in the lap of luxury. After graduating from the University of Southern California, Robert earned his law degree in 1969 from the University of San Diego.

He joined a small boutique law firm run by two fellow Armenians, where he quickly became a specialist in corporate and entertainment law. Robert had a natural talent for developing friendships and clients.

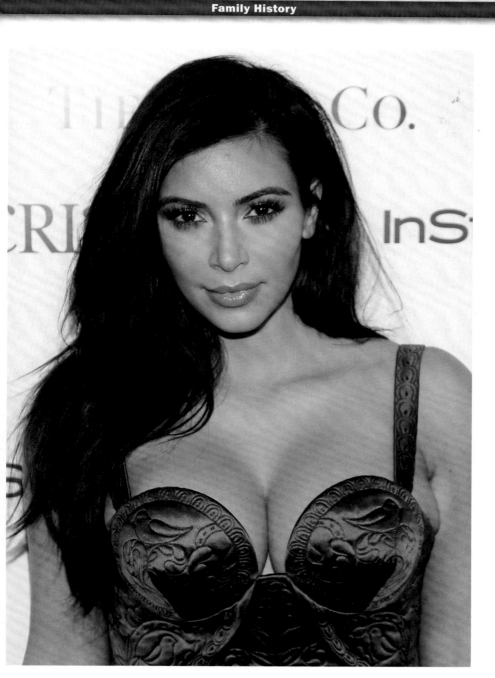

Kim Kardashian comes from a successful immigrant family. The generations before her worked hard to create a safe and lucrative life for themselves in the United States.

One of those clients introduced him to an athlete whose fame would eventually go beyond the playing field: O.J. Simpson. They would become lifelong friends and business partners.

Robert's interest soon moved beyond the law. Along with his brother he founded a trade magazine called *Radio & Records*. The two launched this magazine in 1973. Just six years later, Robert sold his shares for more than $12 million, making him a very wealthy man.

Not all of his businesses were so profitable. One such business, which he opened with Simpson, ended in failure. The business was called Concert Cinema. It streamed music videos to movie theaters before movies began. In the mid 1980s, Robert was named president of MCA's radio network. By this time he had stopped practicing law and was a full-time entrepreneur— an interest and talent that would be inherited by his daughter Kim.

Robert was good looking and successful and an obvious catch for any young woman living in Southern California. One afternoon at Del Mar Race Track, he saw an eighteen-year-old woman who was there with a friend. He approached her to talk and then asked if she would give him her phone number. She refused and walked away. But Robert was not discouraged. That brief conversation had convinced him that she would soon be his wife.

The Future Kris Kardashian

This woman's name was Kristen Mary Houghton. She was born in San Diego, California, in 1955. Her parents, Mary Jo Shannon and Robert Houghton, divorced when she was seven years old. The next year, Kris, her younger sister, Karen, and her mother moved to Claremont, California, to live with her maternal grandparents, Louise and Jim. They had just opened up Candelabra, which was one of the first stores in California dedicated to selling nothing but candles. It was a remarkable success. Kris and her mom both helped at the shop. Eventually, the store's profits helped Mary Jo open up a children's clothing boutique not far from the candle store.

Growing up, Kris worked at both stores and saw firsthand that to achieve financial success one needed to work hard, put in long hours, and pay attention to details. It was a lesson she has used to make herself and her family successful and rich beyond their wildest dreams.

Kris decided college wasn't for her, but was still eager to explore what life had to offer. When she was just seventeen years old, she dated a PGA golfer who was seventeen years her senior. It was he who introduced her to the

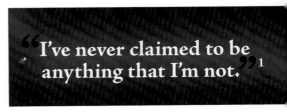

I've never claimed to be anything that I'm not.[1]

world of show business, parties, and yachts—what some would call living the good life. In fact, it was through him that she made many of the connections that helped pave the way to her life today.

She was still dating the golfer when Robert Kardashian approached her at the racetrack. And despite her initial refusal to give him her number, he tracked her down, using his connections to get her unlisted number. The

Why All K's?

Kris has said that when she gave birth to her first daughter, she loved the name Courtney, but she wanted it to be different so she decided to name her Kourtney. Kim got her name because her mother liked they way Kimberly and Kourtney sounded together. With the pattern set, each succeeding daughter was also given a first name starting with K.

two began seeing each other. After Kris officially broke it off with the golfer, their romance quickly heated up.

Kris admits that she was immediately attracted to Robert's great personality. She told a documentary film crew that she knew from the first time she met him that he was going to be the man for her.

But things did not go smoothly. Robert introduced her to his family and asked her to marry him after just three weekends together. The timing was bad. Kris had just gotten the opportunity to become a flight attendant with American Airlines and would be based in New York City. She turned him down, hoping he would wait for her.

He didn't. Instead, he started dating Priscilla Presley, the widow of the King of Rock and Roll himself, Elvis Presley. When Kris read about it in the tabloids, she was heartbroken and wondered if she had done the right thing. Robert's relationship with Priscilla didn't last, though. After a year of separation, when Kris was transferred back to Los Angeles, Robert was waiting for her at the airport in his Rolls Royce.

Kim's father, Robert Kardashian, dated Priscilla Presley during the year Kris lived in New York to pursue her career. As soon as Kris returned to Los Angeles, the two reconciled, marrying in 1978.

Their relationship quickly picked up where it had left off, but one thing had changed. While he had always been religious, Robert had now become a born-again Christian. He kept Bibles on both his desk at work and his nightstand at home. Kris soon joined him in his reborn, strengthened faith. Finally, on July 8, 1978, the two married.

O.J. Simpson was Robert's groomsman, and Al Cowlings, who would become famous years later for driving O.J.'s Bronco during the infamous police chase, was the ring bearer.

Kris's life immediately changed. Robert insisted that she quit her job as a flight attendant and focus instead on becoming a full-time wife and mother. That happened in short order. On April 18, 1979, just nine months and two weeks after marrying Robert, Kris gave birth to Kourtney Mary Kardashian. And just a year and a half later came daughter number two: Kimberly Noel Kardashian, who was born on October 21, 1980.

Growing Up Kardashian

· · · · · · · · · · · · · · · · · · · ·

For Kris Kardashian, now twenty-four with two kids, motherhood was an overwhelming experience. Robert was reluctant to spoil Kris and, at first, would not hire a nanny to help with the children. But he gave in not long after Kim was born.

This is not to say that life was difficult for Kris or the kids. They were living on Tower Lane, a cul de sac so private that there were only three mansions on the street: one owned by the Kardashians, the second owned by Bruce Springsteen, and the third rented by Madonna.

And while the family was still not known, they became famous in the area for giving the best parties. Their mansion came with all the requisite luxuries: a large swimming pool, a Jacuzzi, and a poolside bar. There was a housekeeper to do the

"Everything is better with a K. Klassy with a K!"[1]

Kim and Madonna

Kim has always been a huge Madonna fan, even dressing like her when she was in high school. And, for a time while the children were growing up, Madonna also lived next door to the Kardashians. On one occasion, she gave the girls some of her old rubber bracelets and bangles. The girls brought them to school and told people that they were gifts from Madonna— but nobody believed them!

shopping and laundry, which gave Kris the chance to get out and see her friends. "Uncle" O.J. Simpson would come by to play tennis on a weekly basis; weekend barbecues were a regular feature, attended by family and famous friends alike.

The Glamorous Life

While this life was normal to Kourtney and Kim, it must have seemed like heaven on earth. Kim's father affectionately called her Kimbo and also Joge, which in Armenian means "imagine." The two girls, so close in age, were inseparable friends and shared a bedroom despite living in a mansion. They even wore the same outfits often.

They had pets galore: cats named Coco and Chanel after the famous French fashion designer; a dog (one of many) named Valentina, who died after accidentally eating poison—an event that broke Kim and Kourtney's hearts; rabbits; and birds.

Of course, sisters being sisters, Kourtney loved embarrassing Kim whenever she could. On one occasion, while they were looking at a magazine, she asked Kim if she knew the names of the models. She didn't of course, so Kourtney pointed at various ads for jeans and told her that one model wass named Jordache and another was named Calvin. When Kourtney's friends came to visit, she would ask Kim to name all the models, which she proudly did—not knowing that she was actually reciting the brands of the jeans instead! And soon there were

The Kardashian brood grew to include Khloé, Kourtney, Robert, and Kim. Also pictured are Kris and Caitlyn (formerly known as Bruce) Jenner, Kris's second husband and stepfather to Robert's kids.

more kids. Khloé Alexandra was born on June 27, 1984. And on March 17, 1987, a long-hoped-for son named Robert Arthur (after his father and grandfather) was born.

Despite the glamorous lifestyle they were living, religion was still very much a daily part of their lives. Robert would lead the family in grace before meals and usually had a Bible on hand. Bedtime stories were a mixture of traditional fairy tales and stores from the Bible.

When the girls began going to the exclusive Buckley School, their circle of famous friends got even larger. These friends included Paris Hilton, Nicole Richie, T. J. Jackson (the nephew of Michael Jackson), and Allison Azoff (now Statter)—Kim's best friend to this day.

"[I took] my first selfie in 1984."[2]

The daughter of music mogul Irving Azoff, Allison avoids the spotlight as much as Kim seems to seek it out. The two are rarely photographed together, but Kim still remains closer to Allison than any of her more famous friends. She has said on countless occasions that the day she met Allison was the day she was born.

The Kardashians were, as they say, living the dream. But that dream was about to come to an end.

A Marriage Ends

While Robert and Kris seemed to be a happy couple, behind the smiles Kris was unsatisfied. She was missing the passion she had felt for Robert in the early days of their marriage.

She found that passion in the arms of a man ten years her junior. Their affair lasted for two years. Robert learned about it after hiring private detectives to follow his often missing wife. After an incident in which Robert attacked the car Kris and her lover were riding in with a golf club, he moved out of the house and filed for divorce.

Despite what was going on between them, Robert and Kris wanted what was best for the kids. They agreed that to avoid disruptions, Robert would stay at the family's house every other weekend and Kris would stay at a friend's house.

Then they sat the kids down to tell them the news. Khloé and Rob were too young to understand, but Kim and Kourtney were devastated. Kris has said that knowing what she did to them is the single biggest regret of her life.

For Kim, who loved both her mom and her dad, it was a painful experience. Hearing her mother cry after

Kim's Treatment of Khloé

When they were growing up, Kim took great pleasure in tormenting her younger sister Khloé. She has said that she loved to dress her up, pick her up, and carry her around like a doll—no matter how much she cried and screamed. Why? In part, Kim has said, because of her need to be the center of attention.

fighting over the phone with Robert was deeply upsetting. Kris has said that on one occasion, after a particularly brutal argument with Robert, Kim found her crying. Kim was so upset that she called her mom twice that day from school, hysterically crying and begging to be allowed to come home.

On top of that, Kim was experiencing the normal difficulties of entering adolescence. Kim has said that, at the time, she wasn't as bothered about the divorce because her anxiety was focused on what was happening to her own body, in particular the size of her rapidly growing breasts. As she says in *Kardashian Konfidential*:

> I was mortified that they were growing so much. I got a lot of attention from the older boys in school, which made me feel uncomfortable . . . I remember sitting in the bathtub and crying, putting hot washcloths over my breasts to try to shrink them. I literally prayed to God, "Please don't let them grow any bigger."[3]

Of course, Kris would try to reassure her. She told her to just wait and that the time would come when she would be happy with her curves. And mom was right. Now Kim embraces and is proud of her curves.

The normal pains of growing up combined with her parents' tough divorce were bad enough. But life with the Kardashians was about to get even worse.

Dramatic Changes

. . . .

It was a difficult time not just for Kris but also for Kim, Kourtney, and the entire family.

Not only was Kris going through a divorce, she was also facing an uncertain financial future. Angry at Kris's betrayal, Robert had cut off all financial support, including cancelling her much-loved credit cards. At her lowest moment, she was so broke that when she took the kids out for pizza one night, she realized she didn't have enough money to pay for it.

In time, Robert's bitterness towards Kris faded and they were able come together for the good of the children, to act as parents, and even to become friends.

But for Kris, this period, marked not only by a bitter divorce but also by the news that her mother, Mary Jo, was battling cancer, was the most painful of her life.

She was horrified by the mistakes she had made. She had thrown away the love of her husband Robert and the life he had provided for her and her family for a fling with a younger man—a fling that ended when she found him cheating on her with another woman.

Kris had long seen herself as a woman committed to strong family values, to her religion, and to her family. But by her actions she had ended her marriage and in the process had hurt the man she now realized was the greatest guy in the world—Robert.

She knew something would have to change. She needed to get a grip on herself and get her life back where she wanted it to be.

Starting Over

Then she met Bruce Jenner (who is now know as Caitlyn, since transitioning to a female) on a blind date.

Jenner had won the Gold Medal in the 1976 Summer Olympics in the decathlon. Good looking, funny, and sweet, Jenner was twice divorced with four kids; Kris was divorced with four kids. The Olympian was a religious conservative with strong family values; so was Kris. They were both ambitious.

Kris would later say she and Jenner fell in love on that first date.

Kim immediately accepted her mom's new partner. She often tells the story of Jenner suggesting she do an assigned school project on Bruce Jenner. After Kim asked why, Jenner sat her down and explained about the Olympics and the decathlon. Jenner even came to school with Kim to help present it, which guaranteed an A for Kim and her lifelong love for a person who would become very important to her.

In this iconic photo before her transition to Caitlyn, Bruce Jenner celebrates victory at the 1976 Summer Olympics. Jenner's gold medal made her a star and a celebrity known around the world, long before becoming known as Kim Kardashian's stepdad.

Kourtney was a different matter. She resented Jenner taking her dad's place and at first would only wear black when Jenner was around. But she too eventually accepted the situation.

One thing still stood in the way of Kris and Jenner's relationship: Kris's ongoing divorce battle with Robert, which was now in its eighteenth month. Jenner decided it was time to take charge, meeting Robert at Hamburger Hamlet for a discussion and dinner.

Jenner told Robert that he wouldn't have to pay Kris anything and that she, Jenner would handle all of Kris's finances. Sign the papers and it would be over.

Robert did and it was.

Kris and Robert Kardashian's divorce became final in March of 1991, four months after Kris and Jenner had announced their engagement. One month later they married, in the presence of all their children, and a modern-day Brady Bunch family was created.

The new family moved to Malibu, which allowed Robert to move back into the house on Tower Lane. Kris and Robert's relationship became friendly; The Jenners would often have dinner with Robert and his new girlfriend, Denise Halicki, sometimes accompanied by O.J. Simpson and his beautiful young wife, Nicole Brown Simpson.

Teenage Concerns

Life for Kim returned to normal as well, helped by Robert's insistence on still playing a major role in her life. He drove her and her siblings to school whenever possible and took them to church on weekends. He even gave Kim a Bible that he had he signed to her, making it one of her most valuable and treasured possessions.

She had a large circle of friends, but she and her closest friends shared their own form of sign language so they could talk about people who were in the room without them knowing it.

She also displayed a growing interest in clothes. On many mornings, Kim and Kourtney did not have time to eat breakfast because it took them so long to get dressed and ready for school.

Kim was also showing a passion for making and creating beautiful things, especially jewelry. She collected every type of bead imaginable and would spend hours going through them, finding just the right ones to make a particular necklace, bracelet, or earrings.

As she entered her teen years, however, the quiet studious girl began to turn into the livelier girl one imagines when hearing the name Kim Kardashian today. This new Kim made a public appearance after her eighth grade graduation, when she was filmed at a party by another student.

> "Back in the day, I thought I had the best style. I look back at outfits and I'm like, mortified."[1]

In the film, a more grown-up looking Kim is seen dancing before speaking into the camera: "Is anyone getting a tape of this? I hope you do, because see me when I'm famous and old, you're gonna remember me as this beautiful little girl." She continues as the cameraperson walks away, "Excuse me, are you leaving? My name's

Kim Kardashian. I'm the dopest of the ropest person in this class. I'm dope on a rope."[2] Not only was she the dopest of the ropest, but at this time she also had her first serious boyfriend, Michael Jackson's nephew T.J.

Kris's New Role

While Kim was becoming a teenager, her mom was trying to revive her new husband's career.

Following her Olympic win, Caitlyn was seen everywhere—magazine covers, TV shows, and even in a movie featuring musical group the Village People, titled *You Can't Stop the Music*. But that soon ended and by the time Caitlyn met Kris, Caitlyn was said to have just $200 in the bank and to be more than $300,000 in debt. It would be up to Kris to make Caitlyn a champion again and rebuild both her reputation and her bank account.

She put together a press kit and got Caitlyn jobs, many of them as a motivational speaker. They worked together to make a workout video called *Superfit with Kris and Bruce Jenner*, which they sold through endless

Kim's Dream of Being a Reality TV Star

While Kim has said she always dreamed of being a wife and mother, she also, truth be told, dreamed of being a reality TV star. When *The Real World* came on, she told friends that when they grew up, they should send in an audition tape. Coincidentally, her show *Keeping Up with the Kardashians* is produced by the same company that produced *The Real World*.

television infomercials that made the family a good deal of money.

It was Kris's first time in front of the camera, and she loved it. It was also the beginning of the Kardashian empire, which would soon involve Kim and every other available family member.

A Murder and a Car Chase

Life had settled down to some kind of normalcy. Kris and Caitlyn had purchased a new home not far from Robert's house. Kourtney and Kim began spending more and more time at their dad's, taking advantage of the quiet to study.

Just ten minutes away from Robert's house was O.J. Simpson's mansion. On June 13, 1994, Robert Kardashian received word that Nicole Brown Simpson, the ex-wife of his friend O.J., had been murdered. He immediately called Kris to let her know; she was supposed to have lunch with Nicole that same day.

Robert did not hesitate to support his friend of twenty-three years, offering to let him stay in his home to escape the media. Four days later, Robert stopped his friend from killing himself in the bedroom Khloe used. None of the girls were aware of just how bad things were with O.J.

After a warrant was issued for O.J.'s arrest for the murder of his ex-wife, his chief attorney, Robert Shapiro, asked Kardashian if he would join the legal team. He knew how much O.J. trusted Robert Kardashian. Robert agreed to do it and reactivated his law license in order to do so.

Robert was still concerned about his friend's state of mind and was even more so when O.J. disappeared instead of turning himself in to the police for questioning. He seemed to have made a run for it, heading to Mexico in a white Ford Bronco driven by mutual friend Al Cowlings.

Meanwhile Robert Kardashian spoke to the press on O.J.'s behalf, reading them a handwritten letter that

Robert Kardashian became known to the general public in his role as part of O.J. Simpson's defense team. His support for Simpson caused a rift within his family.

30

O.J. had left at the house before making his great escape. Kardashian believed that this letter was a suicide note.

Simpson's Bronco run is perhaps the most famous and strange car chase in history, with police vehicles, helicopters, and the media all in pursuit of the white Bronco as it traveled down the highway at 35 miles per hour (56 kilometers per hour). An excruciating ninety minutes later, Simpson returned to his home and surrendered to authorities. It is said that this was the exact moment when the lives of the Kardiashians changed. Kim and her family were now known for being the children of the famous attorney, Robert Kardashian. In fact, there are some who argue that the Kardashians would not be where they are today without O.J. Simpson.

The Trial of the Century

By the time the trial began in January of 1995, Kim was starting to become known outside her immediate circle. Not only was she dating one of the Jacksons, but her father was also on television every day with the most talked-about person in the country—O.J. Simpson.

But the trial caused a major division within the family. While Robert was doing everything he could to keep O.J. from going to jail, Kris was certain that he was guilty. As for Kim, she was convinced that her dad was the smartest man in the world. Since he believed wholeheartedly in O.J.'s innocence, so would she.

Thirteen at the time of the murder, Kim later said about the trial:

> Kourtney and I would go to the trial with our dad and
> we'd sit on one side and I remember looking over and

seeing my mom was on the other side sitting next to Nicole's parents and there was so much tension. If we're siding with this one, then my mom and Caitlyn were upset and if we sit there then my dad is upset.[3]

Everyone in the family chose sides, and Simpson's acquittal on October 3, 1995, did not help to bring the family together. When the girls came home and said they knew he hadn't done it, Caitlyn sat them down to explain that just because O.J. was found not guilty that didn't mean he didn't do it. She then went on to say that she didn't want to hear O.J.'s name in their house again.

Privilege with Limits

Even through all this, Kim (or Kimmy as she was known then) was a relatively normal high school girl. She was not a true party girl, but she enjoyed hanging out with friends and with her boyfriend T.J. And while all of the popular girls in her group were thin and blonde (and she was the exact opposite), she was confident in her beauty and idolized Jennifer Lopez, whose dark and sultry looks, body type, and well-rounded rear end were her ideal.

And like any young girl, when she turned sixteen, her thoughts turned to driving. Her first car was a white BMW, presented to her by her father along with a contract. By signing that contract, Kim agreed to drive her younger brother and sister wherever they need to go whenever the need arose, to run errands for her dad, to not talk back to her parents, to promise to keep her grades up, and to never take drugs, smoke either cigarettes or marijuana, or get drunk.

Knowing that Kim was living a life of great privilege, Robert was determined to instill in her a sense of responsibility. Unlike most of the girls in her class, she wasn't allowed to have a personal credit card. She was only allowed to use her credit card to buy gas, with the understanding that she would have to make all the payments on the card, wash the car once a week, and be responsible for any and all repairs necessary.

Of course, the inevitable happened. One day while driving slowly in bumper-to-bumper traffic, Kim leaned down to pick up the lipstick she had dropped and rear-ended the car in front of her. There wasn't a lot of damage, but when the driver of the car she hit saw the name Kardashian, she was sued for a lot of money.

To pay for it, Kim took a Saturday job as a part-time shop assistant at a local clothing boutique named Body. She enjoyed working around the latest fashions, and she particularly liked the money she earned.

Kim the Neat Freak

Kim Kardashian is a self-confessed neat freak and control freak. Even today, when she gets up in the morning she makes her bed and can't leave the house if it's a mess. And while she doesn't enjoy vacuuming, taking out the garbage, or mopping floors, she loves doing laundry and is very proud of her folding expertise.

A Knack for Fashion

She used her natural instincts for fashion to help her mom, as well. Kris and Caitlyn were shooting infomercials for different companies. Kris's outfits, however, did not meet Kim's standards, so she took charge. She chose the workout clothes for an infomercial about fitness equipment. She chose a smart-looking suit for an infomercial that required business clothes. For Kim, the work was fun and easy.

She was also good at it. So good, in fact, that the company hired her to be a stylist for other infomercials, as well. It was a great experience for Kim. She learned not only how to dress others, but also to dress herself; she learned how to choose clothes that make the best of your good features while taking attention away from the features you're not so proud of.

Her next step, a small but important one, was to start designing items herself. She made colored headbands that she would sell to small boutiques in and around Hollywood.

During this period, she also became the older sister to Kris and Caitlyn's children: Kendall Nicole, born on November 3, 1995, and Kylie Kristen, born on August 10, 1997.

With so many kids around, it seemed like a good opportunity for Kim to make a change. She went to live full-time with her father. She continued to work at Body and helped her father out in his various business ventures—all of which helped prepare her for her entrepreneurial life to come.

But while she might have been prepared for a life of business and even celebrity, nothing could prepare her for Damon Thomas.

A Marriage and a Mistake

Damon Thomas, a record producer, was ten years older than Kim. He quickly swept her off her feet, introducing her to the exciting Hollywood music scene. She moved out of her father's house and in with Thomas without telling her parents what she was doing. Although Kris was suspicious when Kim drove up to the family house in a new Jaguar sports car, she trusted Kim to make her own decisions and said nothing.

In retrospect perhaps she should have. On January 22, 2000, without the knowledge of her parents or family, Kim married Damon. She kept the marriage secret for three months, only telling a few close friends, but the word got out. One of those friends told Kourtney, who went online, got a copy of Kim's marriage certificate, and showed it to their mother.

Kris's initial reaction when she learned the news was anger. But, while not happy about the marriage, she decided to support her daughter as best she could. She believed Kim was old enough to make her own decision.

Robert, however, was not nearly as accepting and refused to speak to her for some time. And while Kris did her best to accept Damon as part of the family, when the time came for her to write her autobiography, she did not name him by name and simply called him "the husband."

Record producer Damon Thomas secretly married Kim Kardashian in 2000, when she was only twenty. The much-older Thomas proved to be controlling and abusive, and the couple divorced in 2004.

The marriage was not a happy one. After less than two months, Kim quit working at Body on Damon's insistence—he was afraid she would be in contact with old boyfriends. She later said that he wouldn't let her leave the house unless she told him where she was going and with whom. She also claimed that he wouldn't let her go to the mall by herself or hang out with friends and tried to convince her that her mother and sisters were evil.

Determined to make her marriage work, Kim looked for something she could do at home or while working at her father's office to earn extra income. She turned to an unlikely place—eBay.

The online auction site had been launched in September 1995. Kim was quick to see its potential. A huge fan of Manolo Blahnik shoes, which were popularized both by the TV show *Sex and the City* and her idol J.Lo, Kim came up with a marvelous idea. With a loan from her father (complete with the usual contract agreeing to pay the money back with interest), she bought five pairs of the shoes, similar to the ones Jennifer Lopez wore, for $750 each. She then put them up for sale on eBay, where each pair sold for $2,500, earning her a cool profit of $9,000. After this, she began to take anything from her wardrobe that she was no longer wearing and put it up for auction. A smart business person sees an opportunity and then runs with it.

But while she was successful on eBay, her marriage was a failure. The couple separated in early 2003 and divorced the following year. Kim claimed that Damon had physically abused her on more than one occasion.

It was a painful experience for her, but one she learned from. She later told Matt Lauer on the *Today Show* that, "You think you know so much about love when you're young and you look back later and probably realize it's not what you thought it was."[4]

And in her book, *Kardashian Konfidential*, she talked about what she learned: "I've always been afraid to hurt people's feelings . . . I stayed with guys too long when they weren't treating me right. I wish I had listened to my parents. When no one in your family likes a person, there's got to be something to it."[5]

And if a failed marriage and divorce weren't enough for a young woman to deal with, while all this was going on, tragedy struck. Kim learned that her father was dying.

Becoming Kim Kardashian

· · · · · · · · · · · · · · ·

In July of 2003, Robert Kardashian announced to his family that he had esophageal cancer. The esophagus is the tube that carries food from the mouth to the stomach. For years he had suffered from chronic acid indigestion and, along with his Bible, always carried antacids with him.

The disease moved quickly. He had a difficult time eating and lost a large amount of weight. Kim stepped in to do what she could to help, making his favorite cereal, Cream of Wheat topped with extra sugar, every morning. It was something she had done for him when she was a little girl and now did again as a twenty-two-year-old woman. She hoped to make his last days easier. He died on September 30, 2003.

Shortly after the funeral, Kim planned a getaway vacation to Mexico for her twenty-third birthday. The night before she left, she made a video recording of herself engaging in intimate acts with her boyfriend.

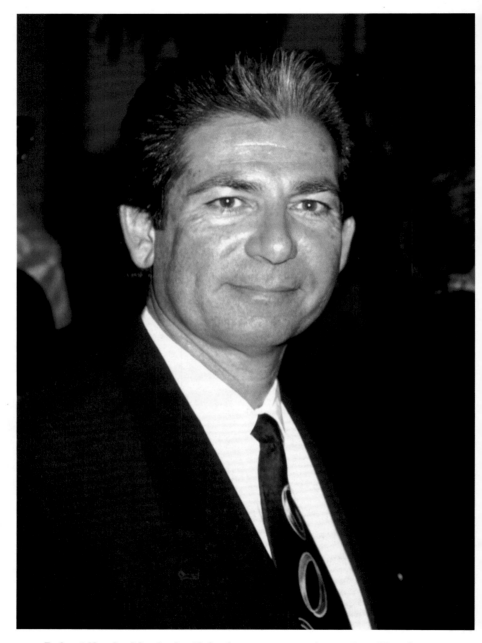

Robert Kardashian's death had an enormous impact on Kim, but so did his life. He worked hard to teach his children the value of hard work, family, faith, and helping those less fortunate.

Lessons from Robert

What did Kim learn from her father? Among other things, do not forget where you came from. Work hard and always give your all. Never drink, do drugs, or smoke. Have fun, be silly, and pull practical jokes whenever possible. Save your money. And, maybe most important, be a good person.

Although it was just supposed to be for the two of them, the tape would eventually have a remarkable effect on her life and career.

Her boyfriend was a rapper and actor named William Ray Norwood Jr., known as Ray J. He is the brother of singer and TV actress Brandy. In fact, Brandy introduced them to each other while Kim was working for her, another step on her road to becoming Kim Kardashian.

Closet Queen

Kim was able to earn some income by buying and selling on eBay, but it wasn't enough to satisfy her. She put her organizational skills to work, helping friends and celebrities go through their closets, organize everything, and sell what wasn't needed on eBay.

She became known as the "Queen of the Closet Scene." Celebrities from Cindy Crawford to Rob Lowe began using her services. From there, she moved on to being Brandy's personal stylist. Her responsibilities

Kim learned a lot from friend and employer Paris Hilton about how to leverage one's fame into a successful career. The hotel heiress became nationally known as a reality TV star and socialite.

ranged from picking up dry cleaning to recommending clothes for Brandy to wear.

When Kim worked with Brandy Norwood, the star was married and expecting her first child, which became the topic of Brandy's first reality TV show *Brandy: Special Delivery*. It was eye opening for Kim to learn firsthand that it was possible for someone to live their normal life and have it filmed and then aired as entertainment. Throughout her life, Kim has been a quick study. She is a natural at learning from others, then doing it even better.

And after she learned all she could from Brandy, she moved on to learning from Paris Hilton, who helped make Kim Kardashian's career possible.

Inspired by Paris Hilton

Paris, who had gone to preschool with Kim, was a pop culture phenomenon. Tall and blonde, Paris Whitney Hilton was a part of American high society—her great grandfather, Conrad Hilton, had founded the Hilton chain of hotels. Paris used her famous name and looks to become a celebrity of the first magnitude—famous for being famous.

She modeled. She dated Leonardo DiCaprio. Gossip columns featured stories about her on a nearly daily basis. A famous photo of her in hot pants was featured in *Vanity Fair* magazine—a lesson for Kim on how something as simple as a photograph can be used to gain the maximum amount of publicity. And she also learned that publicity earns more publicity and any publicity makes one more famous.

Even bad publicity can make one more famous. Paris had signed on with her sister Nicky to star in a reality television series called *The Simple Life*. In it, the socialites would be sent out into the real world to work on a farm for example or live with a family in the South. The network thought that audiences would love the idea of watching Paris, who had never had a real job, mingle with regular people.

But before shooting could begin in December of 2003, an explicit sex tape Paris had made with her then boyfriend two years earlier for their own enjoyment was released for sale to the public. It was made available by the former boyfriend, who initially sold it on his own website. He then went on to make a distribution deal with a large company, earning millions of dollars from it. Paris was, naturally, furious at his betrayal of her privacy. She sued and is said to have settled for $400,000 in addition to a share of the profits, most of which she donated to charity.

> I always learn from my mistakes but something like a photoshoot, I never regret. [1]

In the firestorm that surrounded the release, Paris held her head high and moved forward. She knew what she had done was nothing to be proud of, but she accepted the reality of the situation and moved on.

Her sister Nicky dropped out of the TV series. Nicole Richie, the daughter of pop singer Lionel Richie, took her place. The show was a hit, and Paris did not hesitate to take advantage of it: she recorded an album, wrote a bestselling book, acted on other TV series, launched her own perfume and jewelry lines, and made hundreds of thousands of dollars making personal appearances.

Kim was by her side throughout this period. She worked as Paris's assistant, organized her closets, accompanied her to clubs, and even appeared briefly on *The Simple Life*. And all the while she was learning the ins and outs of how to be famous and make money doing so.

But she was still unknown. Until May 24, 2006, that is.

Discovered by the Paparazzi

After an afternoon screening of the movie *The Da Vinci Code*, Kim was photographed by paparazzi leaving the theater with Nick Lachey, lead singer of 98 Degrees. He had recently broken up with his wife and reality show costar, Jessica Simpson.

The next night, the tabloid photographers were out in force, looking to get more pictures of the woman Lachey was dating. As Kim wrote,

> I was out with Paris Hilton and we were going to a club on Sunset. We were in her car and paparazzi started taking pictures. Usually they would shout, "Paris! Paris! Paris!!" But the night before they'd gotten these pictures of a mystery girl with Nick and by then they'd figured out who I was. So they started yelling out, "Kim! Kim!" I wanted to hide, and Paris and I looked at each other and just laughed. She said, "Whatever you do, just smile. And don't say anything under your breath because they now have video camera too." I thought, "This is so weird. I don't know what's going on." It was surreal.[2]

Kim and Social Media

Before there was Twitter, Instagram, and Facebook, there was Myspace. And Kim was there as well, using the name Princess Kimberly. After acquiring 856 friends, Kim saw the importance of social networking as a tool for self-promotion. As her Myspace bio read, "I'm a Princess and you're not, so there."

That surreal moment would soon become her reality. All day, every day, 365 days a year.

But one question remains: how did the paparazzi know she was going to be at the movies with Nick Lachey? He claims that nobody followed them, but then, somehow, there were thirty photographers waiting for them when they left. Did someone tip them off? It is all a question of playing the game.

And in early 2007, the game became very real.

A Private Moment Goes Public

Rumors started to spread publicly that a sex tape of Kim and Ray J existed. In February, Kim appeared on the TV show *Extra* as a correspondent covering New York Fashion Week. In that same episode, Kim confirmed that the tape did exist.

Not only did the tape exist, but it would soon become available to the public. Vivid Films, a company that made a name for itself by distributing celebrity sex

Kim Kardashian and her boyfriend William Ray Norwood Jr., better known as Ray J, had already split up by the time their privately made controversial sex tape made Kim a household name.

tapes, announced that it had purchased the tape from an undisclosed third party for $1 million and would release it online and in stores on February 28, with the title *Kim Kardashian: Superstar*.

And with that, the media frenzy surrounding Kim Kardashian began in full force.

After Vivid made its plans known, Kim Kardashian issued a statement announcing her plans to sue the company:

> This tape, which was made three weeks ago and was meant to be something private between myself and my then-boyfriend is extremely hurtful not only to me, but to my family as well. I am filing legal charges against the company who is distributing this tape since it is being sold completely without my permission or consent.[3]

The company's chairman, Steven Hirsch, quickly responded, arguing that they had the legal right to distribute the video. He went on to say that he hoped that both Kim and Ray J could work with the company for the good of all involved.

The case never went to court. Less than two months after Kim filed suit, Vivid released a statement that the two had reached a settlement: "We met with her several times and finally reached a financial arrangement that we both feel is fair . . . we always wanted to work something out with Kim so she could share in the profits."[4] It is said that the settlement included a $5 million payment to Kim, as well as a deal that allowed Vivid to distribute the tape as planned.

The uproar over the tape made Kim virtually a household name, and the timing couldn't have been better.

A Shrewd Business Deal

It was at this time that Kris Jenner approached Ryan Seacrest, the host of *American Idol* and president of his production company, about the possibility of creating a reality TV series. The series would record the life of her large combined family. It would focus on the dating, romantic, and personal lives of the girls, particularly Kim, who was now one of the most talked about young women in America.

Many people found the timing suspect. Did Kim arrange the release of the tape in order to give her career a boost in the same way that the release of Paris Hilton's similar tape had boosted hers? And why would she reach an agreement with Vivid that allowed the video to be released in the first place?

The answer to the first question remains uncertain. While Ray J and others have said things that leave the impression that Kim was somehow involved in leaking the tape, she has always denied it. She told the *New York Daily News,* "I'm not poor; I'm not desperate. I would never attempt to sell the tape. It would humiliate me and ruin my family. I have two successful businesses, and I don't need the money."[5]

But the answer to the second is clearer. By reaching an agreement with Vivid (some say with Kris's help and advice), Kim was able to control the video's distribution (which would have happened regardless) as well as keep some of the earnings for herself instead of them all going to Vivid.

It was obviously an unfortunate situation for all concerned. But as Kim has done throughout her life, she realized her mistake, made the best of it, and used it to her best advantage.

And by doing so, she became a television star and celebrity of the first magnitude.

Keeping Up with the Kardashians

·····························

V arious members of the family had tried without success to make it in the world of reality television. Kourtney had been featured in the show *Filthy Rich: Cattle Drive*, which sent her and nine other children of wealthy parents to face the wilds of Steamboat Springs, Colorado. The show was not a success.

Caitlyn Jenner had been a contestant on the show *I'm a Celebrity . . . Get Me Out of Here!* It also was not a success. Even Brody and Brandon Jenner, Caitlyn's sons from her second marriage, had starred in their own reality series called *The Princes of Malibu*, in 2005. That, too, was not a success.

None of those failures was enough to stop the Kardashians from trying again. But whose idea was it to put the lives of the entire family on screen?

Kim and Power Naps

Kim loves to nap. So when she's on a photo shoot or the like and everyone else goes to lunch, she uses the opportunity to take a nap. Once in Las Vegas, she had several events lined up for one evening. So she attended the first, went back to her hotel to change, went down to dinner and before the main course was served she excused herself, went back to her room, took a fifteen-minute nap and returned to dinner. Everyone thought she'd just gone to the bathroom!

Reality TV Beckons

Kim and her sisters credit the idea of making a reality tv show to a family friend and star of the *Today* show, Kathie Lee Gifford. In their book *Kardashian Konfidential* they say that whenever Gifford would visit she'd tell them that they were such a crazy family that there should be cameras on them at all times. Kris obviously agreed. After she pitched the idea to Ryan Seacrest, he dispatched a camera crew to film a family barbecue to get a sense of what the family was like.

Seacrest later told *Haute Living Magazine*, "I remember perfectly. [The cameraman] called me from their house and said, 'It's absolutely golden; you're going to die when you see this tape. They're so funny, they're so fun, there is so much love in this family, and they're so chaotic—they throw each other in the pool!'"[1]

Seacrest loved what he saw and took it to E! Entertainment Television to see if they were interested in the show. Initially, Lisa Berger, E!'s vice president of programming, wasn't sold on the idea. But after Seacrest showed her the tape, emphasizing Caitlyn Jenner's role in the show (at this point she was still the best known member of the family), Berger agreed to sign the show. It would be produced by Bunim/Murray Productions, which had made a name for itself producing reality shows like *The Real World* and Paris Hilton's *The Simple Life*. What the show still needed was a title.

Legend has it that the title came about when someone on the show's production team arrived late at a meeting. This person apologized by saying, "I'm sorry I'm late. I'm just having a really hard time keeping up with the Kardashians."

Filming began on April 21, 2007, and it wasn't long before the media began reporting that the star of that controversial sex tape was going to be featured in a reality television show. But that wasn't enough to promote the show, so promotional material emphasized Kim's friendship with Paris Hilton, as well as the fact that she was Caitlyn Jenner's stepdaughter.

As filming progressed, all concerned became convinced they had a hit on their hands. Watching the footage, it was clear that the Kardashians were, in their own way, a real-life sitcom. Caitlyn Jenner was there to play the role of the conservative parent, Kris was the wacky mom, Khloé was the smart, wise-cracking sister, and Kim was the beautiful quiet one. Everyone, in essence, played a role.

53

Khloé, Caitlyn, Kim, Kris, Kourtney, and Robert attend the premiere of *Keeping Up with the Kardashians* in 2007. The show brought them fame and fortune beyond their wildest dreams.

• • • • • • • • • • • • • • • • • • • •

The show debuted on October 14, 2007. As difficult as it might be to believe this today, audiences had no idea what to expect at the time. The Kardashians as a family were still basically unknown, except that Caitlyn Jenner had been an Olympic star more than thirty years earlier and Kim's sex life had become news.

So the first episode was the family's introduction to America. The tone was set in the very first scene, when Kim is seen bending into the refrigerator to find something and disparagingly refers to her "junk in the trunk." Of course, Kim's "junk in the trunk" would quickly become one of her greatest assets.

> "Even when I was a little girl ... all my friends would be like, 'Oh, my god, your butt's so big.' And I'd say, 'I love it.'"[2]

Later in the same episode, viewers watch as Kim prepares for an interview with model and TV star Tyra Banks, where she knows there are bound to be questions about the tape. Kris then speaks directly to the camera. She admits that when she heard about the tape, as Kim's mother, she thought about killing her daughter. As her manager, however, she knew she had a job to do and used the tape to further her daughter's career. Kris Jenner has said that her job is to take her kids's moments of fame and make them last as long as possible. And by using the sex tape to its best advantage, she essentially turned lemons into lemonade.

The fourth episode of the season shows Kris at her best, helpfully pushing Kim to make a decision she might not have made on her own; one that propelled her to even greater levels of celebrity. It opens with Kris, in her role as manager (or "momager" as she describes herself, a term she later trademarked) taking a call from *Playboy* magazine asking if Kim would be interested in posing nude for their celebrity issue. Kris heads out to meet Kim and tell her the good news. "They really, really, really, really want you to do it," she tells her daughter. "Wouldn't it be fun?"

Perhaps not surprisingly, Kim isn't sure if it would be fun. She tells the camera that ever since the scandal over the sex tape, she feels it's necessary to be extra careful with her reputation and how the public sees her. Kris on the other hand sees no problem, telling the camera that doing it would be an awesome experience and adding, "On top of all that, it's a ton of money."

Kim worries that she will be known only for nude videos and photos and that her fans will wonder if she can do anything else. Kris pushes her, telling her that the shoot will be "classy" and says in no uncertain terms that Kim should do it, because it will "be really great." Kourtney points out that Kris, as Kim's manager, has a financial incentive to encourage Kim to do it. She says, "Of course you want her to do it, with your ten percent commission."

After much back and forth between various Kardashians, Kim agrees to do the shoot. And as in most television shows, there is a happy ending. Kim is happy with the photos, and Kris, challenged by her daughter, does a shoot of her own, dressed only in an American flag with Caitlyn's gold medal around her neck. She presents this picture to her husband as a present at the end of the episode.

Public Reaction

It is perhaps at this moment that the Kardashians, and Kim in particular, became a pop culture phenomenon. People across America discussed and argued about the Kardashians and, soon enough, the rest of the world joined in. People couldn't get enough of the Kardashians, particularly, it seemed, the mother-daughter team of Kris and Kim. Where else could one watch a mom try to convince her daughter to pose nude for *Playboy* magazine?

Despite this, critics of the series were not kind. One, Amaya Rivera of *Popmatters*, wrote:

> [Paris] Hilton's former pal Kim Kardashian, whose claim to fame is a sex tape she made with D-list R&B singer Ray J, and whose father Robert Kardashian got his 15-minutes of fame as one of the O.J. Simpson trial lawyers, is the latest of these dubiously talented wealthy girls to get her own reality show . . .
>
> As far as plot goes, it's hard to imagine anything more boring. Kim, Khloé, and Kourtney, all in their late 20s, pal around, argue and fight with one another, and occasionally with their brother Rob—and that's about it. They take care of and probably negatively influence their 12-year old half sisters Kylie and Kendall, while their mother Kris (notice all the K's!) plays best friend to all of them, living it up with the three older girls in Vegas, for example, while [Caitlyn] Jenner plays the [comedy] straight man, continually befuddled by the wackiness around [her] . . .
>
> There is something a bit disturbing about the Kardashians' intense hunger for fame. But even worse— it is downright boring to watch this family living out their tedious lives.[3]

Critics may not have been impressed, but audiences quickly fell in love with the show. By the time the *Playboy* magazine episode aired, it had become the most popular Sunday night show for women aged eighteen to thirty-

Kim Kardashian and football player Reggie Bush enjoyed a high-profile romance. Their relationship would end in 2010, largely because of their devotion to their careers.

four, with a total viewership of 1.3 million. Naturally, it was picked up for a second season.

A High-Profile Romance

Not only was Kim Kardashian one of the most talked about people in the country, she was also dating again—this time a famous athlete.

His name was Reggie Bush, a star running back for the New Orleans Saints football team. They had met in 2006 at the ESPY sports awards. He was twenty-one, and Kim was twenty-five and a recent divorcee. He didn't ask for her number that night; it was months before they finally went on their first date, when they met at a carwash before going for dinner at a local Mexican restaurant. But by spring of 2007, their relationship went public.

The pairing was a potent one, and they quickly became one of the top celebrity couples in Los Angeles.

Their relationship was difficult: Kim was working in California on *Keeping Up with the*

> I think it's more of a challenge for you to go on a reality show and get people to fall in love with you for being you. [4]

Kardashians and Reggie was living in New Orleans six months out of the year. She visited him often. Despite the glamorous façade she presents to the public, in her personal life, she enjoys staying in. She and Reggie played board games and watched television in bed.

Kim and the Paparazzi

Kim has what she refers to as a love/hate relationship with the paparazzi—those photographers who follow her every move. Sometimes, of course, they show up when she least expects it, so she knows she has to look her best anytime she goes out and must always have sunglasses with her—just in case.

Although Kim was not previously a fan of football, she showed an interest in the sport for her boyfriend's sake— but she only watched football games in which Reggie was playing. Her new boyfriend returned the favor by agreeing to be filmed as part of *Keeping Up with the Kardashians*. He didn't much enjoy having the cameras following him around but allowed it for Kim's sake.

Taking Advantage of the Moment

Kim was busy with far more than her TV series. Encouraged by her mother, she was determined to take advantage of her new star status and explore every offer she received. She appeared in a rather strange video for the Fall Out Boy single "Thnks fr th Mmrs" from their album *Infinity on High*. With the exception of the band and Kim, every character in the video was played by a chimpanzee!

She appeared in the film *Disaster Movie*. In this movie, a group of reality television stars, including Kim,

Kim Kardashian was teamed up with Mark Ballas on the popular television competition *Dancing with the Stars*. Much to her disappointment, she was the third contestant to be eliminated.

have to contend with a meteor strike that will destroy the world. The reviews for the film were uniformly awful, but Kim did manage to receive her first award nomination—a Razzie for WORST Supporting Actress of 2008. And while she took the "honor" with good humor, it must have been an odd experience and a relief to lose to her former bestie, Paris Hilton, who won for *Repo: The Genetic Opera.*

She agreed to appear on the popular television series *Dancing with the Stars,* which at the time was America's top-rated show with 15 million viewers weekly. Unfortunately, Kim had scant dance experience and was not naturally gifted in that regard. While she looked great and was teamed up with the reigning professional champion Mark Ballas, Kim was the third contestant to be eliminated, lasting only one week on the show. She accepted her defeat graciously, saying, "Every dance was a huge accomplishment for me, and I did the best I could."[5]

She recorded a single and filmed a video to accompany it. But even with the involvement of such heavy hitters as The-Dream, Hype Williams, and Kanye West, it was far from a success. The *New York Daily News* said bluntly that based on the recording "Jam (Turn It Up)," Kim was the worst singer to ever emerge from reality television. The song barely sold, and the video, for reasons still unknown, was never released. Kim would later confess, "What gave me the right to think I could be a singer? Like, I don't have a good voice."[6]

Along with these temporary career setbacks, her relationship with Reggie had come to an end. The difficulties of a long-distance relationship were simply too much to overcome. At this point in her life, Kim's most important relationship was with her work—and making herself a brand.

In this she would succeed beyond her wildest dreams.

Kim Kardashian the Brand

· · · · · · · · · · · · · · · ·

The brand was the product being sold. While the Kardashian family as a whole was a brand, Kim was seen as the most marketable brand of them all. Kris proved to be the force behind the brand. She saw *Keeping Up with the Kardashians* as a means to build a family business empire. And she was tireless in her efforts to build that brand. As she wrote in her autobiography:

> I realized that if I was going to tackle this whole situation and be there and manage my family . . . [t]here was no way to do this half-assed. I knew I could not do this as a hobby, or part-time, or just a couple of hours a day. This job required that I live, breathe, eat, sleep it 24/7, and once I decided to do that . . . there was no turning back.[1]
>
> Now I had to be the manager, the businesswoman, the television host, and the leader of the pack. I was the one that my family was looking to, asking, "Okay. Mom, what's next?" I had to be so on top of it all, because I didn't want to let anybody down . . . Every six months,

Kim and I would sit down and ask each other, "OK, what are our goals?"[2]

Kim says that she and her mom are very much on the same page when it comes to business and branding. And with the exception of an occasional disagreement, their relationship—both personal and business—is a good one. They are both total workaholics, and, as Kim admits, they could both work on

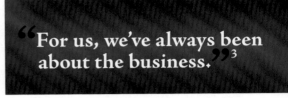

"For us, we've always been about the business."[3]

Christmas and it wouldn't bother them in the least.

How to Become a Brand

The first element of branding Kim Kardashian was basic: sell an image of Kim to the world that would appeal to a wide audience. In this, the Kardashians were lucky. Where Paris Hilton's image was that of a wealthy socialite

Kim's Favorite Foods

Anyone whose fame rests in large part on his or her body knows that what he or she eats is important—and Kim is no exception. After working out, for example, she loves a banana and peanut butter smoothie. Breakfast is usually something like scrambled egg whites with mushrooms and tomatoes and a side of turkey bacon. Lunch and dinner are something simple like a salad or grilled chicken. But for a treat? A cheeseburger and fries!

From the beginning, Kim's brand depended on her approachability. She loves to show appreciation for her fans and has been known to stop to talk and sign photographs for hours.

• • • • • • • • • • • • • • • • • • • •

party girl, Kim's image, based on real life, was that of a nice, approachable, hard-working girl with solid family values.

She was also seen, despite her wealth and beauty, as relatable and welcoming to her fans. She is known for signing autographs and posing for selfies for hours on end, often not stopping until one of her sisters drags her away!

Kim has said on countless occasions that she loves her fans, in part because she knows what it's like to be one herself. When she finally had the chance to meet her idol Jennifer Lopez for example, she was nervous and worried that J.Lo would turn out to be different than she imagined. But she couldn't have been nicer. And that is exactly how Kim wants to be for her fans. "One time in Las Vegas right after our fashion line came out," she remembers, "I saw literally five girls wearing outfits from the line, I was so excited and waving at them, wanting them to come talk to me. I like being myself; I don't want to be unapproachable."[4]

Part of what makes Kim so approachable is her honesty about who she is. She talks openly about the mistake of the sex tape, about her romances, and about her issues with her body image. She's open about her love of food and her refusal to diet just to fit into some ideal body type. She's proud of her curves and proud of her body image. She has spoken out about the emphasis of super skinny girls in ad campaigns, saying it sets unrealistic expectations in young girls.

Social Media Savvy

Kim Kardashian was a brand that sold, and Kim took every advantage of the situation. Early endorsements from ShoeDazzle and Famous Cupcakes and a fitness DVD were just the beginning.

She was an avid user of social media, embracing it as a way to directly reach her growing army of fans, while making money at the same time. It was rumored that even at the start of her career, she could earn as much as $10,000 per Twitter announcement and was paid $25,000 by Armani for just one tweet, which sent forty thousand users to Armani's website in less than twenty-four hours. Today, her fee is as high as $300,000 for a single post sponsored by any number of companies who have signed her.

Her early work for Carl's Jr. is a prime example of her business savvy and attention to detail. The chain originally wanted her to be the face of a campaign for a particular burger. But she wasn't particularly good at eating burgers, and, since she was on a low-carb diet, she was the perfect choice for a new salad they were launching.

She tweeted about the salad. She posted about it online. In 2009, she even hosted what was called "The Ultimate Salad Lunch Date," eating a cranberry, apple, and walnut grilled chicken salad while meeting and greeting fans.

Her work paid off. The campaign was said to be more successful than all of the company's campaigns built around celebrities combined. The thirty-second YouTube commercial was viewed 1.8 million times, and the other salad videos she had made garnered an additional 2.1 million views. By the end of the 2010, her followers on Twitter had almost doubled—to more than 5 million. (Today that number stands at an astonishing 58 million and counting.)

That year, Kim explained to the *Hollywood Reporter* how she uses her social media presence to help the Kardashian family's marketing goals:

Breakups and the Media

If you think it's difficult to go through a breakup, imagine having to do it with the world watching your every move. And after several very public breakups, Kim learned that while it was important to be open with her fans, it was also important to try and keep her breakups private for at least the first weeks. That way, she was able to think about it and deal with it before the rest of the world had a chance to gossip about what went wrong.

I have a blog that has 40 million hits a month. People leave comments: "What shoes do you wear, and what lip gloss do you use?" My mom told us, "So why not be a brand for our fans and give them what they want?" Many of our ideas [about what to endorse] come from our fans and then our mother makes it happen."[5]

Expanding Her Empire

In 2010, Kim was selling more than salads. She brought out her own perfume, naturally called Kim Kardashian by Kim Kardashian, which was marketed as "the voluptuous new fragrance." (The fact that Paris Hilton had had great success with her own perfume line, which grew into a $2 billion fragrance empire, might have influenced her decision to try launching her own.)

Kim's perfume quickly became the number one–selling fragrance of the year at the beauty mega-chain Sephora. New perfumes, including Gold, Glam, and

One of Kim's most successful business ventures is her line of perfumes. Here she is seen at Sephora in February 2010 celebrating the launch of her signature fragrance, Kardashian.

True Reflection would follow, earning her over $100 million in the process.

She worked with Loren Ridinger to create a luxury line of earrings for her new jewelry line, the Kim Kollection. She released a line of signature watches. Where there was money to be made, she was there. She was paid just to make an appearance at a club or event. In 2011, Kim was paid between $100,000 and $250,000 to fly in and appear at a club. This rate went up to $1 million for a New Year's Eve appearance.

She told *Cosmopolitan* magazine, "The appearances are good moneymakers. And they're also a great way for me to connect with people in places like Oklahoma, where I never would go otherwise."[6] In fact, the only time Kim does go to a club is when she is paid to do so. While there she doesn't drink and she always leaves before midnight. She's there for the money, to meet her fans, and for nothing else.

She is so relentless in selling herself and her brand that in November of 2010, she even made an appearance in New York City's Time Square for the opening of a public toilet facility.

All her hard work making herself known was paying off. By the end of 2010, she was the highest-earning reality TV star, with an estimated $6 million. But unlike her sisters, she didn't have much of a personal life. Her older sister, Kourtney, was in a long-term on-and-off relationship with Scott Disick. She had a son with Disick, named Mason Dash Disick, in December 2009. His arrival was, naturally, featured on the show. (The two also have a daughter, Penelope Scotland Disick, born in 2012, and another son, Reign Aston Disick, born in 2014.)

Khloé had married NBA basketball star Lamar Odom in 2009, only thirty days after meeting him. Their wedding was filmed for *Keeping Up with the Kardashians* and was the most watched episode in the show's history up to that time, with 3.2 million viewers.

It would take two years for Kim to get married again; this marriage lasted only seventy-two days.

CHAPTER SEVEN

A Horrible Mistake

· ·

Kim was in New York City in late 2010 filming her spin-off series *Kourtney and Kim Take New York*. On the surface the show was about the opening of the sisters' new DASH boutique in SoHo—the successful business's third location—but it really focused on Kim's search for love.

Just before the series launched, she told MTV News, "It's the first time that I'm single. I have never been single in my life. So [after] getting married as a teenager and then getting into a relationship, each lasting, like four years—after that, something inside of me, I just felt like I wanted to be single."[1]

A Marriage Made for TV

Then she met Kris Humphries. An NBA player like her sister's husband Lamar, Kris was 6 feet 9 inches tall, making him a foot and a half taller than Kim, who is only 5 foot 3. (Many people are shocked upon meeting

Kim Loves Robes

If Kim has one major addiction it's that she loves robes. To her, they're the essence of comfort. She owns at least ten of them to change into when she gets home from a long day of work. Her one rule regarding robes: they have to be in light colors. Dark robes are not allowed. In fact, dark towels aren't allowed either—they make her feel dirty!

her at how petite she really is.) She was introduced to Kris, who was playing for the New Jersey Nets, through a mutual friend, Nets point guard Jordan Farmar. She immediately found him attractive, and he found himself drawn to her as well.

After spending New Year's in Las Vegas, Kim flew to Minneapolis, Kris's hometown, to watch the Nets play the Minneapolis Timberwolves. She also had dinner with Kris's family after the game, a sign, perhaps, that she was taking the possibility of a relationship seriously.

And while Kris was also interested in pursuing a relationship with Kim, it seems unlikely that he had any idea that his life was about to change completely. Known previously only by diehard basketball fans, Kris was about to become famous beyond his wildest dreams and his every move would be recorded and photographed.

Curiously, he had never seen *Keeping Up with the Kardashians*. Before meeting Kim he had no interest in the show in the least, describing it to an ex-girlfriend as

While their courtship and wedding was seen by millions on TV, the marriage between Kim and Kris Humphries ended soon after it began, leading many to wonder whether it was done just for ratings.

a bunch of garbage. But within weeks of the beginning of their relationship, Kris became a part of that "bunch of garbage"; television cameras were on hand to record every moment of his courtship of Kim Kardashian.

In the opening episode of the sixth season of *Keeping Up with the Kardashians*, Kim introduces Kris to viewers as her boyfriend. By episode thirteen, he is getting ready to propose marriage.

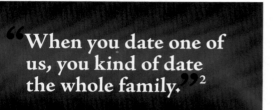

"When you date one of us, you kind of date the whole family." [2]

After asking Caitlyn's permission to marry Kim, he set the stage for the big proposal (unless it was the show's production team that did the work). Entering her Beverly Hills home one afternoon, Kim finds Kris in her bedroom on bended knee. On the perfectly white carpet, in rose petals, he has written, "Will you marry me?" He then shows her a gigantic 25.5-carat diamond ring worth an estimated $2 million—a ring that could grace the finger of the biggest stars in the world. Kim acceptsed the proposal immediately. The question of whether or not they would make a compatible couple is set to the side.

The wedding took place at the Sotto Il Monte estate in Montecito, California. It was the perfect place for Kim's wedding—her idol, Jennifer Lopez, had selected the location for her wedding to Ben Affleck, before their relationship ended and they canceled their wedding plans.

All invited to the nuptials were asked to dress in either white or black. The bride wore an ivory wedding dressed designed by Vera Wang. Caitlyn walked Kim down the aisle. The guest of honor was her ninety-five-year old grandfather, Art, Robert Kardashian's father.

After it was all over, Kim said, "My one regret is that I wish I had more time to really enjoy the wedding, because there's so much going on that you're running around and now that I look, I'm like, 'that day happened so fast.'"[3]

Of course, the wedding was more than just a wedding. It was a media event, a television spectacular, and a money-making, brand-selling opportunity for the whole Kardashian family.

People magazine paid $300,000 for the right to announce the news of the couple's engagement and an extra $1.5 million for the first photos of the wedding. *OK* magazine paid $100,000 for pictures of the bridal shower. *US Weekly* paid close to the same for photos of the honeymoon. And the television network E! paid $15 million for the right to broadcast the wedding as a two-part special.

Although estimates for the cost of the ceremony varied widely—anywhere from $500,000 to $10 million—most of that had been given to the family at no cost in exchange for the publicity. The Vera Wang wedding dress was a gift, as were several hundred thousand dollars worth of flowers. Kim was even paid a $50,000 fee for her bachelorette party in Vegas—negotiated by her mother and manager, Kris Jenner.

The Honeymoon Is Over

It was also momager Kris who surprised the couple with a honeymoon on the Amalfi Coast of Italy. She also made sure that there was a photographer there to take pictures of a bikini-clad Kim cuddling up to her husband.

After the honeymoon was over, work beckoned and signs soon emerged that the marriage wasn't all it appeared to be. On an episode of *Kourtney and Kim Take New York*, after Kris suggests that the couple move back to his hometown Kim asks him, "How am I going to have my career and live in Minnesota?" His response was simple and undoubtedly disturbing to Kim: "By the time you have kids and they're in school, nobody will probably care about you."

Soon after, Kris Humphries was seeing moving his things out of their newly rented NYC apartment. After

Kim's Five Rules for Success

1. Make the most of your opportunities. When you're given a chance, take it!

2. When you do something, dig in and give it your all. Be passionate about whatever it is you're doing.

3. Don't rush into anything. Take your time when you're making a decision.

4. Have a plan. Know exactly what it is you want to accomplish and how you're going to make it happen.

5. Follow through on your commitments.

just seventy-two days of marriage, Kim Kardashian filed for divorce. She issued this statement:

> After careful consideration I have decided to end my marriage. I hope everyone understands this was not an easy decision. I had hoped this marriage was forever, but sometimes things don't work out as planned. We remain friends and wish each other the best![4]

> "My decision to end my marriage was such a risk to lose ratings and lose my fan base. [5]

Whether they remained friends is doubtful; it took twenty months to reach a divorce agreement, far longer than the actual time they were married.

Was the Reality Real?

Just days after the announcement, speculation ran wild that the marriage had been nothing but a publicity stunt. Some said it was a business relationship, not a true love match. Others calculated that the couple had taken in around $250,000 a day over the course of their marriage and asked whether they planned to give back the close to $18 million they had been paid for the photo and TV rights.

On her website, Kim vehemently denied the charges. "First and foremost," she wrote, "I married for love. I can't believe I even have to defend this. I would not have spent so much time on something just for a TV show!"[6] Like every other part of her life, her unraveling marriage was broadcast to the world on that TV show. The second

Eager crowds gathered for the opening of the New York City location of the Kardashian sisters' boutique, DASH. That location has since closed, but DASH Los Angeles and DASH Miami are thriving.

season of *Kourtney and Kim Take New York* gave America an intimate look at Kim and Kris's relationship. A huge audience of 4.5 million were glued to their TV sets for the final episode, which ended with the pair being driven to the airport without a word spoken between the two of them.

It was a difficult time for Kim. Not only was she in the midst of a painful divorce, but also there were signs that the public was turning against her and her family as well. The family's image was under fire by the accusations that the marriage was just a publicity stunt.

Kim was worried that the dream was over, telling *The Drum*:

> At the time when I was going through the divorce I did say to everyone, "You guys I think our careers are over. I hope you've saved your money. And now we'll just continue to do our clothing stores and continue to do what we started off doing before the show." I was being very paranoid. I just took some time off and the time was very good for me. I canceled everything. I had a book tour, I had a fragrance launch, I had everything that you could possibly imagine and I just canceled it all and I took time for me.[7]

But while Kim laid low, Kris Kardashian was busy working behind the scenes, making sure the money kept rolling in. And when Kim emerged six months later, her celebrity would reach even greater heights.

And she'd be with a new man, one whose fame matched hers.

Kim and Kanye

. . . .

Kanye West is one of the most talented and influential rap artists and musicians on the scene today. Kanye and Kim had crossed paths on numerous occasions over the years, but the timing was never right. When one was available, the other was in a relationship and vice versa. Even so, Kim's sister Khloé always said she knew that Kim should marry Kanye.

Legend has it that they first met when he was producing a track he had written for pop star Brandy titled "Talk About Our Love." Kim was working as Brandy's assistant at the time. As the story goes, she made everyone at the session, including Kanye, a cup of tea. But that was as far as it went.

They would meet here and there, but only as friends. Kim has said, however, that there was always a spark. They appeared together in the pilot for a hip-hop puppet show called *Alligator Boots* that was never made into a series.

Kanye dated designer Alexis Phifer for a time. After they broke up, Kim was involved with Reggie Bush. Then when she and Reggie were finished, Kanye was dating model Amber Rose. Despite this, when you hear Kanye's guest rap verse for Keri Hilson's song "Knock You Down," it's not difficult to imagine Kim as the cheerleader and Reggie as the football player:

> You was always the cheerleader of my dreams
> To seem to only date the head of football teams
> And I was the class clown that always kept you laughin'
> We were never meant to be, baby, we just happened[1]

When Kanye walked into the Kardashians' DASH boutique in New York City in October 2010, as seen on *Kim and Kourtney Take New York*, he was once again single. But Kim was just starting her whirlwind romance with Kris Humphries.

Making the First Move

Finally, after Kim had broken up with Kris, the time was right. And it was Kim who made the first move by calling him. Six weeks after the official announcement of her split from Humphries, Kim was seen publicly with Kanye at the after-party for his Watch the Throne tour, where he performed with Jay-Z. Kim was at the party with Khloé, and at the concert she had seats right next to the stage, so Kanye could see her very clearly.

At the party after the show, Kim and Kanye finally got the chance to speak, and those in attendance said they had eyes only for each other. One witness said it was clear that Kanye really wanted to kiss Kim, but there were too many people around.

Shortly after announcing her split from husband Kris Humphries, Kim began dating Grammy Award–winning rap artist Kanye West. They had known each other for years and quickly fell in love.

In March of 2012, Kim joined Kanye, who was also making a name for himself as a fashion designer, at his Paris fashion week show. Being together in Paris, the "city of love," was the start of their real relationship, and she promised him that this time she was ready to make a commitment. Their affair went public at the end of April 2012, when they posed for pictures holding hands at the artist's dinner at New York City's Tribeca Film Festival.

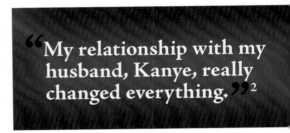

"My relationship with my husband, Kanye, really changed everything."[2]

The couple were moving quickly and made plans to move in together and start a family. Whose house they would live in was an open question, but as Kim told Oprah Winfrey in an interview, "I want babies; I want my forever; I want my fairy tale. And I believe you can have what you want."[3]

In June, Kim bought Kanye a $400,000 black Lamborghini for his thirty-fifth birthday. Of course, she could easily afford to do so; *Keeping Up with the Kardashians* had been renewed for an additional three seasons for $40 million. This was the most lucrative deal in TV history and guaranteed the show would be shown in more than one hundred markets around the world.

And the show, as many in the family happily acknowledge, is primarily a platform from which they can sell their products, of which there are many. In 2011, Kris had signed a deal with Sears to sell a line of affordable clothing and accessories. Two years later, according to *Forbes*, that affordable clothing line had brought in a remarkable $600 million in sales, earning the family at least $30 million.

And then there were earnings from the Kardashian Beauty cosmetics line, book royalties, fees for making personal appearances, and many other endorsements. Kim's take in all this was estimated to be least $28 million. (And momager Kris, who spent up to sixteen hours a day making it happen, earned 10 percent of everything.)

But what the world wanted to know about was the romance, and Kim was happy to oblige by posting on Twitter or Instagram. She knew, being a master of social media, that those posts would then make headlines on mainstream media, increasing her exposure, and making her brand all the more valuable.

On occasion, however, Kanye was the one who made headlines. While performing at a concert in Atlantic City, NJ, on December 30, 2012, he surprised Kim, as well as the audience. Shouting into the microphone, "Stop the music," he pointed at Kim and proudly said, "Can we make some noise, please, for my baby mama right there?"

> "I think God was doing this for a reason. He was saying: 'Kim, you think you're so hot, but look what I can do to you."[4]

Kim made her own announcement on her website the next day, saying: "Kanye and I are expecting a baby. We feel so blessed and lucky and wish that in addition to both of our families, his mom and my dad could be here to celebrate this special time with us."[5]

Kim's Favorite Things

Kim loves fashion magazines. Kim loves inspirational books like *The Purpose-Driven Life* and *Embraced by the Light*. She loves romantic movies like *The Notebook*. She loves recording artists like Beyoncé, Andrea Bocelli, and, of course, Kanye West. And her favorite song is anything by Beyoncé.

Kanye Takes Over Kim's Closet

Ironically, given that one of Kim's earliest jobs was closet organizer, Kanye took it upon himself to take over Kim's closet—and her fashions. He was so excited about the project that even though he doesn't really enjoy being filmed for television, he allowed himself to be filmed doing this for *Keeping Up with the Kardashians*

His goal was for Kim to match his sense of fashion: to become more daring and less conservative. By the time he had gone through her clothes, her closets were nearly empty. Kim agreed, as usual, to put her rejected clothes and shoes for sale on eBay (much of the proceeds from these sales went to help support a new church her family had founded). Kanye then refilled the closet with an entirely new wardrobe, including clothes from his own clothing line as well as other top-name designers.

Growing into Her Beauty

It was indeed time for Kim to upgrade her looks, because, as she admitted on the show, Kanye's interference had landed her on many best-dressed lists.

And designers love working with Kim, especially as the pretty younger woman evolved into a beautiful woman. Sean Smith wrote in *The Daily Mail*:

> There is no denying Kim was born beautiful . . . She is film star beautiful. Hers is a kind of old Hollywood beauty, like a young Elizabeth Taylor. Her features, a gift from the Armenian side of her family, give her enviable blue-black hair, peach-colored skin, and almond eyes. She has that kind of luminous, intense beauty that's impossible to ignore.[6]

And while she is undeniably beautiful, her curvaceous body seems to get the most attention. Most particularly her backside, which is perhaps the most famous backside in the world. It has, indeed, become an important part of her image. She dresses to emphasize this feature and

Kim and Charity

Kim is a firm believer in giving back and has, in fact, donated millions of dollars to the causes she believes in. She supports the Dream Foundation, which grants wishes to adults who are terminally ill. She's given money to the International Medical Corps (IMC) to help those affected in the Philippines by Typhoon Yolanda. She supports the Children's Hospital Los Angeles, not only with monetary donations but by giving of herself as well; she often stops by unannounced to visit the patients, bring them presents, and take selfies with them. She even helped one young girl to do her nails!

makes sure that it is regularly photographed. This means, of course, that there are critics who claim that her rear isn't all natural and that it has been helped along with the aid of butt implants.

Kim felt obliged to prove them wrong, so on a very special episode of *Keeping Up with the Kardashians*, she went to her family doctor (along with her sisters and a camera crew) to get an X-ray to prove once and for all that her rear was indeed all natural. As she said on the show, "Today I am going to have a butt X-ray to prove to the world it's real. This is a really crazy request but my sisters have dared me to get an ass X-ray because of all the rumors it's not real."

After the X-ray revealed her rear was indeed all hers, she said, "I'm so glad I did this X-ray. The whole world has been doubting me—this is the best thing I could've done." And then she pointed at the X-ray of her iconic booty.

In many ways, the move was pure Kim Kardashian. Proud of her body and who she is, she confronted the rumors head on, showed the world who she unashamedly is, and moved on. Many have argued that Kim's positive body self-image and the flaunting of her most famous asset has helped many young girls—and grown women—accept and embrace their own voluptuous shapes.

The Highest Point in Her Life

Kim removed herself more and more from the public eye as her pregnancy progressed. Twelve days after her divorce from Kris Humphries became final, she was rushed to the hospital, saying that something wasn't

Kim and Kanye welcomed daughter North in 2013. The couple have tried to instill their love of fashion in baby North, bringing her along to the front rows of fashion shows early on.

right. It turned out she was suffering from preeclampsia, a condition that affects some women in the late stages of pregnancy, causing extremely high blood pressure. The only cure is to deliver the baby as quickly as possible.

So five weeks earlier than expected, on June 15, 2013, Kim gave birth to a baby girl. She was not, however, given a name beginning with a K. Instead, much to the pleasure of critics, she was named "North," which refers to "highest power." For Kim, giving birth was the highest point of her life.

Perhaps even more surprisingly, the birth was not filmed for *Keeping Up with the Kardashians*. Kourtney had already given birth on the show—twice—and Kim decided that it was time for her to keep her private life just a little more private. Indeed, she and Kanye (often referred to as "Kimye") did not even negotiate a price for the first pictures of baby North.

Privacy, however, does have its limits. With a healthy baby onboard, Kanye knew the time had come to propose marriage to Kim, and in the most public of ways. After consulting with Kris, who talked him into filming the occasion for *Keeping Up with the Kardashians*, Kanye made his plans. He kept Kim and the rest of the family totally in the dark. All concerned were asked to come to the home of the San Francisco Giants, the AT&T Park, on October 21, 2013.

That night, Kanye took a blindfolded Kim by hand out to the center of the ballpark. Kim, who thought it was going to be an over-the-top birthday celebration, was stunned when, still blindfolded, she heard fireworks along with a fifty-piece orchestra playing Lana Del Rey's song "Young and Beautiful"—her favorite.

When she was finally allowed to take off her blindfold, she found Kanye in front of her. He was smiling on bended knee and holding out an engagement ring while fireworks spelled out "Pleeease Marry Mee!" What else could she say but "yes"?

Wedding of the Century

As preparations for the wedding began, Kim had finally lost the 50 pounds (23 kilograms) she gained during her pregnancy and was looking her most beautiful. She was helped, of course by Kanye, who was always on hand to help her look her best; a necessary task if one's business is selling oneself and one's brand.

She looked so beautiful, in fact, that she was invited to appear on the cover of *Vogue* magazine in May 2014. For the photo, she wore a wedding gown with her ring prominently displayed, with Kanye behind her holding her in his arms. One of the world's great photographers, Annie Leibovitz, took the picture. The result was an iconic photo of the happy couple.

The wedding and preliminary celebrations were held in Europe. Events began in Paris, where Kim and her best girlfriends met for a fitting of the wedding gown and a private dinner (filmed of course for *Keeping Up with the Kardashians*). At the dinner, her mother's best friend, Shelli Azoff, offered a toast that gave the world a glimpse of how her family and friends saw the real Kim outside the public persona:

The wedding of Kim and Kanye made headlines worldwide. Here, the couple, besieged by fans, leave their hotel for their pre-wedding celebration at a castle at Versailles on May 23, 2014.

• • • • • • • • • • • • • • • • • • • •

There are things I look for in people. And the big thing for me is heart, loyalty, and most of all character. Kim possesses all of those . . . I am incredibly proud, and always have been, of who you are as a human being, as a person. I am incredibly proud of how smart you are. I am incredibly proud of how kind you are. I am incredibly proud of where you are today and I love you very much.

The celebrations then moved to Florence, Italy, where, on May 24, 2014, Kim and Kanye were married in the sixteenth-century Forte di Belvedere. As Kim walked down the aisle on the arm of Caitlyn Jenner, she heard the voice of one of her favorite singers, Andrea Bocelli, singing "Ave Maria." As they said their vows, one hudred white doves were released into the sky. At the reception, John Legend sang "All of Me."

Setting the tone for it all was the bride herself, who was radiant with happiness. Fashion commentator Alison Jane Reid wrote, "The dazzling white of the gown gave her a look of extraordinary radiance and contrasted brilliantly with her dark hair and black eyes . . . she looked luminous, elegant, timeless and as regal as a royal bride."[7]

Kim Kardashian West was now nearly thirty-five years old—happily married, a doting mother, and rich, successful, and famous beyond her wildest dreams.

Little did she know that she was about to become even more successful. And that a family secret she had been keeping for nearly ten years was about to become very public.

Success Beyond Belief

• •

By 2014, Kim Kardashian had, through hard work and a masterful use of social media, made herself rich and famous beyond belief. She had seized upon every business opportunity that had come her way—fashion, jewelry, and television. And in June of 2014, she launched one of her most successful ventures ever.

Kim the Game

Kim became a mobile mogul with the introduction of her iPhone and tablet game, *Kim Kardashian: Hollywood*. The concept is simple: players create their own Kim Kardashian–like character, and as they play, the character rises to ever greater fame and fortune.

It was in the summer of 2013 when Niccolo de Masi, the CEO of Glu Mobile, approached Kardashian with the idea. Kim told *Forbes* magazine, "I loved videogames, growing up. I remember I asked Kanye, 'Should I do this?' He was like, 'Yes!' That's how he got into music, because he wanted to do music for videogames and wanted to create videogames."[1] But she had her doubts and wondered if people would really want to play a game that mimicked her life.

For Kim, the opportunity to control her own virtual character was irresistible. By year's end, she and de Masi had come to an agreement with the assistance of momager Kris. Kim would have editorial approval, be able to finalize all clothing ideas, and sign off on every storyline in the game. According to Kim, she signs off on "every single outfit, to the eyeliner, to the hairlines, to the color tones."[2] (De Masi says that she responds to his texts faster than any of his own employees.)

Kim said that she was overwhelmed by the positive comments from her fans. And when the game brought in $74.3 million in just its first six months, she knew she was on to something big. "When I found out what my percentage was," she said, "I was like, 'Oh, my gosh.' Then I was like, 'Okay, whatever we've got to do to keep this going.'"[3]

Is Kim the World's Highest Paid Writer?

Consider this: Kim Kardashian earns up to $300,000 per tweet! Each tweet is made up of 140 characters, with an average of ten or so words per tweet. Divide ten into $300,000, and you can see that Kim is paid $30,000 per word!

In 2013, Kim expanded her resume to include "mobile mogul" with the launch of *Kim Kardashian: Hollywood*. The game earned her $45 million in its first two years.

• • • • • • • • • • • • • • • • • • • •

The business model for making money on this sort of game is simple: give the game away for free, and then make money through all the in-app purchases that increase the quality of the game and help keep it new.

Kim used her celebrity and giant social media presence to maximize sales. She did this by aligning real-life events in her life with the game's virtual events. She had the game characters go to Punta Mita, Mexico, for example, on the same day that Kim herself arrived for a vacation. "The whole idea," she told *Forbes*, "was to make it feel as live-time as possible. I would give [Glu] bikinis

> "I love when people underestimate me and then become pleasantly surprised."[4]

> What is my talent? Well, a bear can juggle and stand on a ball and he's talented, but he's not famous. Do you know what I mean? [6]

and be like, 'Hurry up and mock up this bikini,' because I'm going to wear it, and then you can have it in the game!"[5] By matching up Kim's real-life travels with those of the virtual characters, the possibilities for earning money were virtually endless.

The game brought in a staggering $160 million in its first year, earning Kim a spot on the cover of one of the nation's leading business magazines, *Forbes.* In response, she posted the following on Instagram: "Such a tremendous honor to be on the cover of @forbes! I never dreamed this would happen & know my Dad would be proud. #NotBadForAGirlWithNoTalent."[7] Her dad, who had encouraged entrepreneurship in his daughters, would indeed have been proud.

Bruce, Caitlyn, and Kim

Even as her family had thrust itself into the public eye, with cameras following their every move, they were harboring an important secret. Kim had kept silent about it for more than ten years. One day she had came home earlier than expected and found Caitlyn alone in the house wearing a dress. She was so surprised that she ran out of the house without listening to Caitlyn's explanations. She never told a soul.

Since she is known as the "Queen of the Selfie," it made sense that Kim would assemble a book of her favorite selfies, appropriately titled *Selfish*.

Caitlyn's secret was a big one, one that had weighed on her for her entire life. As most secrets do, it eventually came out. What was this secret? Her gender identity did not match up with the gender she was assigned at birth. This means that although Caitlyn was designated a boy when born, she identifies as a woman. She felt like a woman and saw herself as a woman. Caitlyn is a transgender woman; her gender identity does not match her assigned birth gender. And it was a secret she kept to herself for a very long time.

Circumstances change, however, and so did Caitlyn. Her marriage with Kris went through tough, stressful times. Despite twenty years of a marriage that appeared successful from the outside, the couple split in June of 2013. In a statement, they announced that they were now living separately, they would always love and respect each other, and their family would always be their number one priority.

Kim and Transgender Issues

Since Caitlyn transitioned, Kim has used her fame and celebrity to draw attention to the plight of transgender men and women who aren't lucky to enough to have the same support from their families that Caitlyn has. Rates of suicide attempts among transgender men and woman are as high as 40 percent. Kim has spoken out about the need for acceptance.

Kim proved to be the most supportive of all the Kardashians when Caitlyn publicly transitioned. Above, Kris, Khloé, Kendall, Kourtney, Kim, Caitlyn, Kylie, and little North attend an event together.

A seemingly liberated Caitlyn, now nearly sixty-five years old, knew this was the moment to become who she truly was. She made an appointment for a surgical procedure to lessen the size of her Adam's apple—often the first step in gender affirmation surgery.

Unfortunately the news went public before Caitlyn was ready to announce her transition. This sent her into a brief period of despair. But when her divorce from Kris was finalized, she knew the time had come to tell her family and the world the news.

The well-respected journalist Buzz Bissinger wrote an article for *Vanity Fair* magazine in which Caitlyn revealed her new identity for the first time. Annie Liebovitz, the same photographer who took Kim's stunning cover photo for *Vogue*, took photos for the article.

Caitlyn appeared in a two-hour *20/20* special with journalist Diane Sawyer, where she announced to the world, "To all intents and purposes, I am a woman."[8] It would be the last interview she would give under her former name.

The Kardashian side of his family did not appear for the interview (that would happen on *Keeping Up with the Kardashians*, of course). However, Caitlyn did say that Kim had been the most accepting and easiest to talk with about the transition. Her words of advice? "Girl, you gotta rock it, baby. You gotta look good."[9]

Interestingly, it was Kanye West who helped Kim accept and adjust to her stepparent's new reality. Caitlyn spoke about it during the interview: "He said to Kim, 'Look, I can be married to the most beautiful woman in the world and I am. I can have the most beautiful little daughter in the world and I have that . . . But I'm nothing if I can't be me. If I can't be true to myself, they don't mean anything."[10]

Two months later, the *Vanity Fair* issue appeared. Caitlyn had transitioned. The cover proclaimed, "Call Me Caitlyn"—and there she was in a stunning photograph that belied her sixty-five years. Kim met Caitlyn Jenner for the first time at that photo shoot. "She's beautiful," she told *Vanity Fair*, "and I'm so proud that she can just be her authentic self. I guess that's what life is about."[11]

And as Kim's life and success have proven, being your own authentic self is exactly what life is about.

Keeping Up
with Kim

· · · · · · · · · · · ·

The year 2015 was busy for Kim Kardashian for many reasons, not just because of the launch of her video/mobile game or the media frenzy of her step-parent's transition.

In January, she premiered a thirty-second commercial for T-Mobile Data Stash during the Super Bowl. In February, she and her family signed a reported $100 million deal that would keep *Keeping Up with the Kardashians* on the air with E! for another four years. (The show is currently seen in 120 countries.)

In April, she honored the memory of her father by visiting Armenia for the first time, accompanied by Kanye and North. There, she laid flowers at the Genocide Memorial and met with Prime Minister Hovik Abrahamyan. The family went on to Jerusalem, where North was baptized.

Also in April, she was honored by *Variety* magazine's Power of Women Inspiration Impact for her charitable

The Armenian Genocide

During the Armenian Genocide, 90 percent of the Armenian people in the Ottoman Empire were deported and exterminated over the course of World War I (1914–1918). It is a charged subject for Kim Kardashian and her family.

The Turkish government today refuses to acknowledge this shameful chapter in history as a genocide, stating that there was never a formal policy to drive out or eradicate the Armenian people from their lands. And many governments, including the US government, refuse as well for largely diplomatic reasons. However, most historians agree that the mass exterminations and deportations fit the generally recognized definition of genocide. The Armenian people—including Armenian Americans like Kim Kardashian—continue to fight to honor their ancestors as victims of genocide.

work. In May 2015, she announced she was pregnant with her second child and published a book of selfies, titled *Selfish*, which became a bestseller. In June, she was number thirty-three on *Forbes*'s list of the world's 100 highest-paid celebrities.

On December 5, 2015, she gave birth to a son named Saint.

All this in addition to filming her television show, running her various businesses, making personal appearances, and being a wife and mother. For Kim, part

To honor her father and her Armenian heritage, Kim, along with husband Kanye, sister Khloé, and daughter North, traveled to Armenia in April 2015. There, she visited the genocide memorial.

of being a wife is standing up for her often controversial husband. At a live event held at Madison Square Garden in April 2016, Kanye debuted a new track, "Famous." The song includes a line about the possibility of having sex with pop megastar Taylor Swift because, he claims, he made her famous at their infamous 2009 Grammy Award encounter.

Swift went to the press, complaining that the lyrics were inappropriate, that Kanye had in fact talked to her about the song, and that she had cautioned him about releasing it at all. Kanye responded on Twitter, claiming that Swift had not only approved of the song, but that one of the lyrics had been her idea in the first place.

It looked like it was going to be a classic she said/he said argument—that is, until Kim came to the rescue. Thanks to her abiding passion for social media and getting all of her life's events on film, she had actually filmed her husband's conversation with Swift on Snapchat. She released the snaps, which collaborated Kanye's version of the story, and the controversy came to an end.

Terrorized in Paris

She and Kanye have a life that seems like a fairy tale. They live in a home with eight bedrooms, ten bathrooms, eight fireplaces, two pools, two spas, tennis courts, a vineyard, an entertainment center, and a separate guest house. They even purchased the house next door for $2.9 million to help ensure their privacy.

Of course, every fairy tale life has its moments of horror and terror. And Kim's is no exception. On

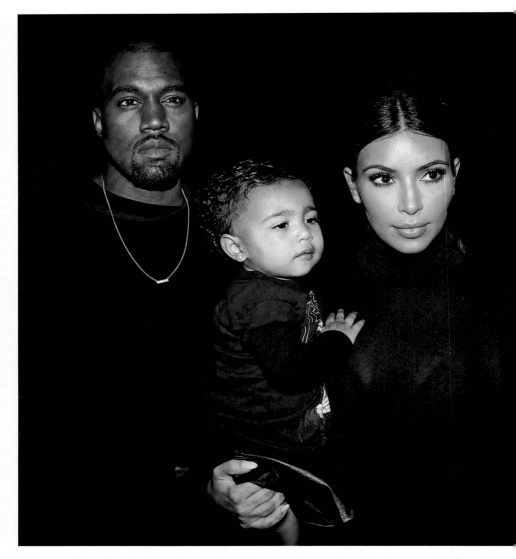

Kim Kardashian is savvier than most people give her credit for, turning herself into a successful brand that seems infinitely bankable, even as her job title has shifted to wife and mother.

October 2, 2016, while attending Paris Fashion Week, Kim was robbed at gunpoint in the apartment where she was staying. Five individuals, all dressed as police officers, bound and gagged her, then stole $10 million worth of jewelry.

The thieves got in to her place by threatening the doorman. Then, once they had accessed Kim's room, they held a gun to her head, tied up her wrists and legs, and wrapped duct tape around her mouth to gag her. They then placed her in the bathtub. She was physically unharmed and reportedly begged for her life. After the thieves made their escape, she managed to get her hands free from the plastic ties around her wrists and scream for help.

Filming for the new season of *Keeping Up with the Kardashians* was placed "on hold indefinitely" immediately

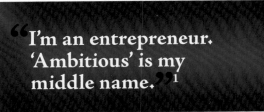

"I'm an entrepreneur. 'Ambitious' is my middle name."[1]

after the robbery, and Kim, at least for a time, pulled back from social media. Why? In part because of the negative comments directed at her on social media about the robbery, and in part to protect herself and her family's privacy. After all, used to a life lived out in the open on social media, Kim had just posted photos of her dazzling jewelry on Instagram. Along with other photos documenting her visit to the City of Light, her social media presence could have made her a target for the thieves.

But despite the ordeal she had been through, with her permission, production of the show resumed on

October 26, 2016. And in true Kardashian fashion, Kim spoke openly for the first about the robbery on *Keeping Up with the Kardashians*.

Kim Kardashian Is a Phenomenon

Over the course of her career, Kim Kardashian has proven herself to be a master of social media and of marketing and merchandising both herself and her brand. She has become, in the eyes of many, famous simply for being famous.

But is that all it is? In a recent interview with *60 Minutes*, Kim said, "It is a talent to have a brand that is really successful and to be successful at getting people to like you for you."[2] When the reporter noted that she's turned being Kim Kardashian into an empire, worth in excess of $100 million, her response, said with a knowing smile, was, "I would think that would have to involve some kind of talent."[3]

And indeed it does. Her earnings from 2016 are estimated at $51 million. And as *Forbes* reported:

> Her *Kim Kardashian: Hollywood* mobile game generated $71.8 million in 2015; some 40% of her annual paycheck comes from her cut of revenue in the game. Add on her Instagram endorsements, the Kimoji app—a $1.99 Kim-based series of emojis—and her $2.99 subscription-based personal app, and Kardashian makes more money from mobile endeavors than anything else.[4]

By moving into mobile endeavors, Kim has proven that she's far more than just a reality TV star, more than the queen of selfies, and more than a face and gorgeous backside. Her image has gone beyond her initial introduction to audiences as a bombshell with a sex tape. She has become respectable and respected, known as much for her business acumen and commitment to her family as she is for her beauty. And her fans have followed her growth every step of the way.

In 2017, Kim and Kanye announced that they were expecting a third child, a girl, via a surrogate mother.

She's a businesswoman and entrepreneur and a wife and mother, for whom nothing is impossible.

1980 Kim Noel Kardashian is born on October 21 in Los Angeles to businessman and attorney Robert Kardashian and his wife, Kris. She joins big sister Kourtney.

1984 Khloé Kardashian is born.

1987 Robert "Rob" Kardashian is born.

1991 Kim is a bridesmaid at her mother Kris's marriage to Olympic decathlon gold medalist Caitlyn (formerly Bruce) Jenner, just four weeks after Kris's divorce from Robert is finalized.

1994 O.J. Simpson is charged with the murder of his ex-wife Nicole. Robert Kardashian renews his law license in order to serve on his friend's defense team. The trial causes a major rift within the family.

1995 Kim's half-sister Kendall Jenner is born.

1997 Kylie Jenner, the last of Kris Jenner's six children, is born.

2000 Kim marries record producer Damon Thomas in Las Vegas without informing her family.

2003 Robert Kardashian dies from esophageal cancer in September. In October, separated from her husband, Kim makes a sex tape with her boyfriend Ray J.

2006 Kim makes her first venture into social media with a Myspace profile using the name Princess Kimberly in January. In May, she has her first encounter with paparazzi; the publication of the photos gets her noticed.

2007 Kim files suit against Vivid Entertainment in February, claiming "right to privacy" regarding the distribution of her sex tape. She reaches a settlement with Vivid in April. *Kim Kardashian: Superstar* becomes the biggest-selling sex tape of all time. That month, filming begins for *Keeping Up with the Kardashians*. The show premieres on E! in October. Less than four weeks later, shooting begins on season two. In December, Kim appears on the cover of *Playboy* magazine.

2008 Kim appears on TV's *Dancing with the Stars* and becomes the third contestant to be voted off.

2010 Kim officially becomes TV's top-earning reality star with $6 million. She launches the Kim Kardashian Signature Watch Collection.

2011 Kim is named Entrepreneur of the Year at the *Glamour* Women of the Year Awards in June. She marries Kris Humphries on August 20. In October, *Kim's Fairy Tale Wedding: A Kardashian Event*, airs as a two-part special on E! Seventy-two days later, Kim files for divorce, blaming "irreconcilable difficulties."

2012 In April, Kim makes her first public appearance with Kanye West at New York's Tribeca Film Festival. She launches a new clothing line for "curvy" girls, the Kardashian Kollection, in November. At his concert in Atlantic City in December, Kanye announces that Kim is pregnant.

2013 North West is born in Los Angeles on June 15. Kris and Caitlyn Jenner announce their separation. In October, Kanye proposes marriage to Kim at the AT&T Park. Kris Humphries sells the engagement ring he gave Kim for $749,000.

2014 Kim wins the Razzie Award for Worst Supporting Actress in Tyler Perry's film *Temptation: Confessions of a Marriage Counselor* in March. She appears on the cover of the April issue of *Vogue*. She marries Kanye West in Italy on May 24. The July release of her video/mobile game, *Kim Kardashian: Hollywood* is an immediate hit, with 28 million downloads and 11 billion minutes of play in just its first six months. In September, she is named as *GQ* magazine's Woman of the Year.

2015 With the rest of her family, Kim signs a reported $100 million deal in February, guaranteeing another four years of *Keeping Up with the Kardashians*. Her book of selfies, *Selfish*, is published in May and becomes an international best seller. She announces she is pregnant with her second child. She meets the transitioned Caitlyn Jenner for the first time. She gives birth to her son, Saint West, on December 5.

2016 While in Paris for fashion week, Kim is robbed at gunpoint in her hotel room; the thieves take $10 million worth of jewelry. She is unharmed.

2017 Kim launches KKW Beauty, her own cosmetics line. Kim and Kanye announce they are expecting a third child, a girl, via a surrogate.

2018 Kim and Kanye's third child, a daughter named Chicago West, is born.

Chapter Notes

Chapter 1: Family History

1. Hardie Grant Books, *Pocket Kim Wisdom: Witty Quotes and Wise Words from Kim Kardashian* (Richmond, Australia: Hardie Grant Books, 2016).

Chapter 2: Growing Up Kardashian

1. Hardie Grant Books, *Pocket Kim Wisdom: Witty Quotes and Wise Words from Kim Kardashian* (Richmond, Australia: Hardie Grant Books, 2016).

2. Ibid.

3. Kourtney, Kim, and Khloé Kardashian, *Kardashian Konfidential* (New York, NY: St. Martin's Press, 2011), p. 31.

Chapter 3: Dramatic Changes

1. Hardie Grant Books, *Pocket Kim Wisdom: Witty Quotes and Wise Words from Kim Kardashian* (Richmond, Australia: Hardie Grant Books, 2016).

2. Sean Smith, *Kim* (New York, NY: Dey St., 2015), p. 52.

3. Ian Halperin, *Kardashian Dynasty* (New York, NY: Gallery Books, 2016), p. 79.

4. Smith, p. 95.

5. Kourtney, Kim, and Khloé Kardashian, *Kardashian Konfidential* (New York, NY: St. Martin's Press, 2011), p. 89.

Chapter 4: Becoming Kim Kardashian

1. Hardie Grant Books, *Pocket Kim Wisdom: Witty Quotes and Wise Words from Kim Kardashian* (Richmond, Australia: Hardie Grant Books, 2016).

2. Kourtney, Kim, and Khloé Kardashian, *Kardashian Konfidential* (New York, NY: St. Martin's Press, 2011), p. 100.

3. Ian Halperin, *Kardashian Dynasty* (New York, NY: Gallery Books, 2016), p. 125.

4. Ibid.

5. Sean Smith, *Kim* (New York, NY: Dey St., 2015), p. 130.

Chapter 5: Keeping Up with the Kardashians

1. Ian Halperin, *Kardashian Dynasty* (New York, NY: Gallery Books, 2016), p. 138.

2. Hardie Grant Books, *Pocket Kim Wisdom: Witty Quotes and Wise Words from Kim Kardashian* (Richmond, Australia: Hardie Grant Books, 2016).

3. Amaya Rivera, Keeping Up with the Kardashians, Season 1, http://www.popmatters.com/review/keeping-up-with-the-kardashians-season-1.

4. Hardie Grant Books.

5. Sean Smith, *Kim* (New York, NY: Dey St., 2015), p. 150.

6. Ibid., p. 153.

Chapter 6: Kim Kardashian the Brand

1. Kris Jenner, *Kris Jenner. . .and All Things Kardashian* (New York, NY: Gallery Books, 2011), pp. 266–267

2. Ibid, p. 271.

3. Hardie Grant Books, *Pocket Kim Wisdom: Witty Quotes and Wise Words from Kim Kardashian* (Richmond, Australia: Hardie Grant Books, 2016).

4. Kourtney, Kim, and Khloé Kardashian, *Kardashian Konfidential* (New York, NY: St. Martin's Press, 2011), p.138.

5. Ian Halperin, *Kardashian Dynasty* (New York, NY: Gallery Books, 2016), p. 156.

6. Ibid, p. 154.

Chapter 7: A Horrible Mistake

1. Ian Halperin, *Kardashian Dynasty* (New York, NY: Gallery Books, 2016), p. 173.

2. Hardie Grant Books, *Pocket Kim Wisdom: Witty Quotes and Wise Words from Kim Kardashian*

(Richmond, Australia: Hardie Grant Books, 2016).

3. Sean Smith, *Kim* (New York, NY: Dey St., 2015), p.173.

4. Ibid., p. 175.

5. Hardie Grant Books.

6. Smith, p. 173.

7. Halperin, p. 198.

Chapter 8: Kim and Kanye

1. Keri Hilson, "Knock You Down," *In a Perfect World . . .*, Interscope, 2009.

2. Hardie Grant Books, *Pocket Kim Wisdom: Witty Quotes and Wise Words from Kim Kardashian* (Richmond, Australia: Hardie Grant Books, 2016).

3. Sean Smith, *Kim* (New York, NY: Dey St., 2015), p. 203.

4. Hardie Grant Books.

5. Sean Smith, *Kim* (New York, NY: Dey St., 2015), p. 203.

6. Sean Smith, "As Kim Kardashian Turns 30," *Daily Mail*, October 21, 2015. http://www.dailymail.co.uk/femail/article-3281027/The-evolution-Kim-Kardashian-star-turns-35-chart-changing-look-personal-assistant-style-icon.html.

7. Sean Smith, *Kim*, p. 218

Chapter 9: Success Beyond Belief

1. Natalie Robhemed, "Kim Kardashian West, Mobile Mogul: The Forbes Cover Story," *Forbes*, July 11, 2016. https://www.forbes.com/sites/natalierobehmed/2016/07/11/kim-kardashian-mobile-mogul-the-forbes-cover-story/#767e40e77e4f.

2. Ibid.

3. Ibid.

4. Hardie Grant Books, *Pocket Kim Wisdom: Witty Quotes and Wise Words from Kim Kardashian* (Richmond, Australia: Hardie Grant Books, 2016).

5. Ibid.

6. Ibid.

7. Kim Kardashian West, Twitter post, July 11, 2016, 8:18 AM, https://twitter.com/kimkardashian/status/752522380119937025?lang=en.

8. Sean Smith, *Kim* (New York, NY: Dey St., 2015), p. 225.

9. Ibid.

10. Smith., p. 226.

11. Smith., p. 228.

Chapter 10: Keeping Up with Kim

1. Hardie Grant Books, *Pocket Kim Wisdom: Witty Quotes and Wise Words from Kim Kardashian* (Richmond, Australia: Hardie Grant Books, 2016).

2. "Kim Kardashian on 60 Minutes: Just Check My Bank Account!" TMZ, October 23, 2016. http://www.tmz.com/2016/10/23/kim-kardashian-60-minutes-social-media/.

3. Ibid.

4. Natalie Robhemed, "Kim Kardashian West's Earnings," *Forbes*, November 16, 2016. https://www.forbes.com/sites/natalierobehmed/2016/11/16/kim-kardashian-wests-earnings-51-million-in-2016/#41e5ef596a5b.

Glossary

acumen Shrewdness.

Armenia A nation located in the mountainous Caucasus region between Europe and Asia. It is the homeland of the Kardashian famly.

entrepreneur A person who innovates or runs a business.

gender identity A person's inner sense of being male or female; it is not necessarily the same as the gender one is assigned at birth.

genocide Deliberate mass killing of an ethnic group in order to exterminate its population.

infomercial A long TV advertisement disguised as an information show.

momager Coined by Kris Jenner, it combines "mom" and "manager."

paparazzi Photographers who earn their living taking pictures of celebrities and selling them to various media outlets.

preeclampsia A condition that can occur during pregnancy resulting in high blood pressure and fluid retention.

reality TV A nonscripted television program, showing the everyday lives of a select group of real people playing themselves.

selfie A photograph taken of one's self, generally on a smartphone or similar device, then often shared on social media.

social media Websites and apps such as Facebook, Twitter, and Instagram that allow users to share photos, videos, and texts with others in their network.

transgender Relating to a person whose gender identity does not match up with the gender they were assigned at birth.

Further Reading

Books

Cohen, Nadia. *Kim and Kanye: The Love Story.* London, UK: John Blake, 2014.

Earl, C.F.. *Kanye West.* Broomall, PA: Mason Crest, 2013.

Halperin, Ian. *Kardashian Dynasty.* London, UK: Simon & Schuster, 2017.

Jenner, Kris. *Kris Jenner...and All Things Kardashian.* New York, NY: Galley Books, 2012.

Kardashian, Kim. *Selfish.* New York, NY: Rizzoli, 2016.

Kelly, Shannon. *Reality TV.* Detroit, MI: Lucent Books, 2013.

Mattern, Joanne. *Kim Kardashian: Reality TV Star.* Minneapolis, MN: ABDO, 2012.

Mooney, Carla. *Caitlyn Jenner.* New York, NY: Rosen Publishing, 2017.

Smith, Sean. *Kim Kardashian.* London, UK: HarperCollins, 2016.

Websites

Kim Kardashian on Facebook

www.facebook.com/kimkardashian

Kim Kardashian's facebook page.

Kim Kardashian on Instagram

https://www.instagram.com/kimkardashian/?hl=en
Kim's Kardashian's official Instagram.

Kim Kardashian on Twitter

https://www.twitter.com/kimkardashian
Kim's Kardashian's official Twitter.

Kim Kardashian West

www.kimkardashianwest.com
Kim Kardashian's official website.

Films and Television

Keeping Up with the Kardashians. Los Angeles, CA: Ryan Seacrest Productions and Bunim/Murray Productions, 2007-present.

Temptation: Confessions of a Marriage Counselor. Directed by Tyler Perry. Santa Monica, CA: Lionsgate, 2013.

Index